POWERFUL PRESENTATION TECHNIQUES

Jack Wolf, Ph.D.

Copyright © 2003 by John M. Wolf & Lifelong Learning Partners
Co-written by Valerie Collins

ISBN 0-9743174-0-3

All rights reserved. No part of this publication may be reproduced, stored in a retrieval system, or transmitted in any form or by any means, electronic, photocopying, recording, or otherwise, without written permission from the author.

Published by Lifelong Learning Partners, Inc., 4115 Pinar Drive, Bradenton, Florida 34210

Telephone: (941) 758-1800
e-mail: jackwolf@ij.net
www.jackwolflearning.com

Contents

SENSORY & PERCEPTUAL LEARNING 1

How we learn
Organizational learning preferences
Right-left brain characteristics
Perceptual processing styles
5 senses
Sensory learning styles
    Visual/Kinesthetic/Tactile/Auditory
    Skills practice

PRESENTATION STYLES 37

Personality styles overview
Presenting from the "Center of the Room"
The four styles

BEFORE YOU BEGIN 47

Theory of Expectancy
Premeeting contact
Voice check (how do you sound?)
Visual check (how do you look?)
Room setup
Presentation tool kit
More points to consider

CREATING SAFETY & OWNERSHIP 59

Socialization
What Board
Encouraging questions
Introductions
When in doubt, write it out!
Language tips
Icebreakers
Tension
Boundaries
Room setup
More tips

HANDOUTS 77
- Why use handouts
- Using visuals
- Layout, design and color
- Best Ideas
- Agendas
- Distribution
- Jargon page
- Implementation (action!) page
- Marketing
- Resources and references

ADDING VISUAL IMPACT 97
- 8-12 second rule
- Creating a visual break
- Multiple visual stimulation
- PowerPoint tips
- Storyboarding and flip charts

PRESENTATION BASICS 107
- Presentation Focus
- Engagement
- Retention Levels
- Brain Breaks
- Auto Pilot
- Powerful Words
- Presentation tips
- Rule of Three
- Primacy and Recency
- Time
- What vs. How
- Jargon
- Question techniques
- Flip charts, 3x5 cards
- Responsible person technique
- WIIFM
- Difficult people
- Closing - "Brain Dump" exercise
- Do You Know?

Contents

REVIEWS 145
   Six Times Rule
   Review techniques
   Reminders/Job aids

ONE-ON-ONE: CLIENT INTERVIEWS 153
   Location and room setup
   Body language
   Boundaries review
   Before the appointment
   What Questions
   Dots and Post-it® flags
   After the meeting

LIFELONG LEARNING PRINCIPLES 167
   Up to Now
   What Is
   Be Here Now
   I Am Enough
   I Don't Know
   I, You, We, All
   From Now On

ADDITIONAL RESOURCES 183

ABOUT THE AUTHOR 185

THANK YOU FOR READING!

Foreword

This book is a combination of tips, techniques and information designed to help you become a better presenter. It is based on the theory that *learning, retention and performance will be optimized by addressing the needs of the learner rather than focusing on your needs as a presenter*. What do your learners need to make this a successful meeting, presentation or training? The human capacity to listen, observe and remember is significantly affected by:

- Physical considerations (room set-up, lighting, participants' health, comfort)
- Socialization needs (who else is in the room)
- Learning and thinking styles
- Stimulation of the 5 senses
- Feelings of safety and ownership
- Personalities (consider not only those of your learners, but your own as well...)

Design your program with built-in "Multiple Opportunities to Learn" (MOL). This allows you to reach every person at least part of the time instead of running the risk of reaching some of them none of the time. What do I mean by MOL? That's what this book is all about - giving you the information and techniques to reach, and really connect with, as many of your learners as possible, in as many ways as possible.

The optimal learning environment is focused as much on the HOW of the presentation as on the WHAT. How are you going to make sure what you have to say, present or teach will be remembered by your learners, audience members or clients? Remember, *technique surpasses content.*

Pre-frame your learners with an awareness of a personal, emotional stake in the learning outcome. Establish a sense of anticipation about the learning. Assess their current level of knowledge before attending and their state of mind once they enter the room. Follow-up assessments should measure application of the information. Application = learning = increased performance.

This book strives to live up to its own lessons by being a user-friendly, easy-to-apply guide for basic and advanced presenters alike, filled with methods and techniques that don't require a huge budget or an advanced degree. As always, your feedback is most welcome and would be greatly appreciated.

To Your Success!

Jack

A picture may be worth a thousand words, but an experience is worth a thousand pictures!

POWERFUL PRESENTATION TECHNIQUES

"Everything should be made as simple as possible, but no simpler."

Albert Einstein (1879-1955)

Chapter 1
Sensory & Perceptual Learning Styles

The purpose of this chapter is to give you some insight into concepts regarding the multitude of factors that affect how your adult learners process, absorb and store new information. This is NOT an exploration of behavioral styles, which assess how adults communicate and express outwardly with others. You will find information on that topic in the next chapter, Presentation Styles. Adult learning concepts focus on how we take in, learn and process the vast quantities of information we receive daily.

Adult learning theory is a widely-researched field and encompasses a diversity of categories and classifications. Each of us processes and retains new information and ideas in a very different way. Understanding the basics of these principles, recognizing similarities and differences within your audiences (customers, co-workers, relatives and friends) will assist you in every area of your life requiring effective communication.

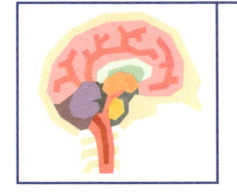

SENSORY and PERCEPTUAL LEARNING

HOW WE LEARN

The following are four predominant methods of receiving and processing information. We learn through our:

- ◆ Organizational learning preferences (right-brained/global or left-brained/linear)
- ◆ Perceptual processing styles (abstract or concrete)
- ◆ Physical senses (touch, taste, hearing, sight and smell)
- ◆ Sensory learning channels (visual, kinesthetic, tactile, or auditory)

Audiences are made up of people with various combinations of learning characteristics and it is up to you to determine how to best deliver your information. Is your audience a combination of preferences or are they predominantly one style?

ORGANIZATIONAL LEARNING PREFERENCES

There are two distinct organizational learning preferences, global and sequential, in which people can be referred to as being either a right-brained or left-brained processor. This refers to how information is organized and processed in the brain.

Global, right-brained processors tend to be creative, artistic, more emotive and are more inclined to see, and want, the big picture.

Linear, left-brained thinkers prefer sequence and logic and organize their thoughts accordingly. They revel in the details and often need someone else to give them the big picture.

SENSORY and PERCEPTUAL LEARNING

Assume you will have both right and left-brained participants in every audience.

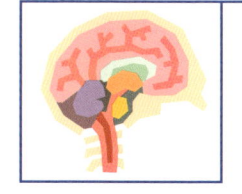

SENSORY *and* PERCEPTUAL LEARNING

The following preferences and characteristics can be attributed to each type:

Right Brain
- Global/Big picture
- Feeler/Emotional
- Intuitive
- Spontaneous/Flexible
- Asks "When...Who?"
- Prefers few or no rules
- Often speaks with animation
- Relationship-oriented
- Unconventional
- Open-ended

Left Brain
- Sequential/Step-by-step
- Thinker/Logical
- Relies on information
- Hesitant/Rigid
- Asks "Why...How?"
- Prefers to know the rules; to have structure
- Level speaking voice
- Task-oriented
- Predictable
- Likes neat endings (closure)

LEFT-BRAINED THINKERS

If you are presenting to a left-brained customer (or a group of engineers) design your session to accommodate them.

- Establish an agenda and stick to it
- Keep the meeting on track and on time
- Distribute reports
- Present the facts; cite examples; use statistics, research, charts and graphs
- Give them time (and enough information) to think things over before making a decision
- Be sure to review the key points before they leave the room

SENSORY and PERCEPTUAL LEARNING

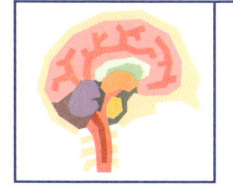

SENSORY and PERCEPTUAL LEARNING

LEFT-BRAINED THINKERS cont.

◆ Keep your emotions under wraps - they are unsettling to left-brainers who may be put off by intensity

◆ Give them a "by-when" time/date for a decision or to complete a project; pin them down to specifics

◆ Give them a task to do or problem to solve

◆ Give clear instructions; set specific goals and outcomes for what you want them to do afterwards

◆ Establish rules, guidelines and boundaries

◆ Persuade them with logic

RIGHT-BRAINED CREATIVES

If you are presenting to a right-brained customer or audience, design your session to accommodate their more creative, free-wheeling tendencies.

- Be prepared to discard your agenda and let the meeting or discussion follow its own course
- Involve them in brainstorming, mind mapping or other creative processes
- Ask for their <u>feelings</u> on the topic
- Global thinkers tend to think laterally and switch from topic to topic at random (at least it seems that way to the left-brained people), linking unrelated facts or solutions with each other

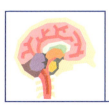

SENSORY and PERCEPTUAL LEARNING

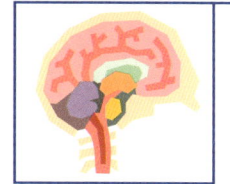

SENSORY and PERCEPTUAL LEARNING

RIGHT-BRAINED CREATIVES cont.

- Use innovative and unusual titles for your programs to pique their interest

- Give the big picture first and then get to the bottom line quickly

- Use a handout that outlines the key points. They will ask for more data if they want it

- Mission and vision (the big picture) are important to right-brained individuals

- Global thinkers are easily bored. Speak in an animated tone, be passionate!

- They may have difficulty actually getting down to the task at hand and moving on from the brainstorming, problem-solving part of the process

    - Quick, intuitive decision makers, they are persuaded with emotion

PERCEPTUAL PROCESSING STYLES

Abstract and concrete can be used to describe the two ways in which people perceive the world around them. This difference is not necessarily tied to either a left or right-brained organizational process, but is how we view and think out about the situations, problems, people, and other things in our lives.

This makes for four distinct thinking styles:

- Left-brained / Concrete
- Right-brained / Concrete
- Left-brained / Abstract
- Right-brained / Abstract

SENSORY and PERCEPTUAL LEARNING

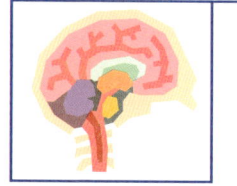

SENSORY and PERCEPTUAL LEARNING

ABSTRACT

Abstract thinkers tend to deal in concepts, theories, and possibilities. They are good with ideas, numbers, emotions, aesthetics, spirituality and other abstractions. They lack interest in specifics but want to know the reasons behind decisions, legalities, the processes involved and how the situation developed. They are comfortable working with words and abstract concepts. They will ask "Why?"

CONCRETE

Concrete thinkers base their thoughts on tangibles - what they can actually feel, see, smell, touch and do. They prefer to work with actual experiences, events, places, things, sounds and colors. They are interested in hands-on solutions, action and specifics. They do best when given application recommendations. They will ask "How?" and "What?"

PHYSICAL SENSES

Touch, taste, hearing, sight and smell. Information filtered through each of these senses affects a different hemisphere of our brain, either the right or left. Only 10% of the learning experience actually occurs through vision. The remaining 90% takes place through touch, perception and other associations.

By stimulating the physical senses, you can keep your audience's/listener's/customer's attention longer and have a greater likelihood of them remembering what your meeting or presentation was all about. Here are a few tips you can use in your next interaction...

SENSORY and PERCEPTUAL LEARNING

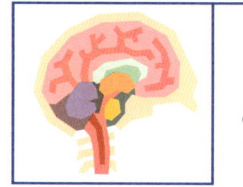

SENSORY and PERCEPTUAL LEARNING

TOUCH Touch or physical contact (hand on shoulder in greeting, handshake, hug, etc.) to the left side of the body is processed by the right brain which controls emotions, creativity and long-term memory. Stimulation on the right side of the body is processed by the left brain which controls logic, reason and short-term memory.

◆ Note-taking, already a left-brained activity (words and numbers), is made even more so when the writer uses his or her right hand, as most do. To increase right-brain activity and long-term memory, engage participants in a mind mapping session, a brief drawing exercise or have them attempt to write temporarily with the other hand. You can let your left-handers know they are *already* more creative than the more ordinary right-handers!

TASTE Our sense of taste stimulates both sides of our brains. Providing light snacks, water or other beverages will wake your audience up before your meeting or presentation.

HEARING Like touch and sight, hearing is cross-hemispheric, meaning that right-side stimulation affects the left brain and left-side stimulation affects the right brain.
- Position yourself on your listener's left side if you want them to store the information in long-term memory.
- Place yourself on your listener's right side to deliver technical or logical data.
- Use music! Soft mood music enhances learning by relaxing the mind. Lively music is good for breaks and energizing your audience.
- Food for thought... Which ear do you usually use when on the phone?

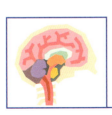

SENSORY and PERCEPTUAL LEARNING

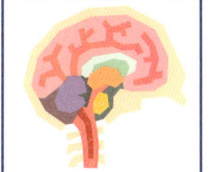

SENSORY and PERCEPTUAL LEARNING

SIGHT Like touch and hearing, sight is cross-hemispheric, meaning that right-side stimulation affects the left brain and left-side stimulation affects the right brain.

- When your customer is ready to make a decision (an emotional response), place yourself on his or her left side to stimulate the right brain.

- To trigger creativity and long-term memory put pictures, logos and other visual stimulators on the left side of your materials (i.e. PowerPoint, handouts, business cards, etc.)

SMELL Our sense of smell is the strongest of the five; the 20 million cells in each of our noses are directly connected to our brains. Make sure the meeting environment is not musty or stale. Fresh air, mild aromas sharpen your learner's (customer's) mind.

SENSORY LEARNING CHANNELS

Information comes to us through four main sensory learning channels. While each of us has one predominant channel through which we prefer to learn, we process and store information through all four channels.

In our culture, most learners are visual, tactile or kinesthetic. Less than 10% of adults have an auditory (listening) preference. So then why are most meetings, sales presentations, and other learning experiences delivered primarily via an auditory experience, i.e. talking or lecturing? Understanding and "speaking" to the different styles can open the way to clearer, more effective communication and increase other people's understanding of what you have to say.

YOUR AUDIENCE MAY NOT "LISTEN" WITH THEIR EARS, BUT WITH THEIR EYES, THEIR BODIES OR THEIR HANDS.

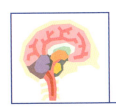

SENSORY and PERCEPTUAL LEARNING

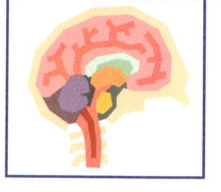

SENSORY and PERCEPTUAL LEARNING

The four primary learning style categories adults* fall into are:

Visual	**40-45%**	**Tactile**	**20-25%**
Kinesthetic	**20%**	**Auditory**	**10%**

Our audiences, customers, co-workers, etc. may have a very different learning style than we do. Try to accommodate all four styles when making a presentation or facilitating a meeting.

KNOW YOUR AUDIENCE

One-on-one meetings: Assess the other person's style by their body language and verbal language cues.

Group meetings/presentations: Assume that all 4 styles are in your audience. **"Sweep"** your audience by presenting to different styles at various times during your presentation. Change the focal point of your delivery method by using a variety of presentation stimulators.

* Children are predominantly tactual and/or kinesthetic up to the age of 12.

PRESENTATION STIMULATORS

When presenting, either one-on-one or to a large group, the following things can be used to stimulate learning in the four styles.

Visual:
Charts/graphs
Flip charts
Whiteboards
PowerPoint
Overheads/slides
Manuals
Pictures
Brochures

Kinesthetic:
Group exercises
Dyads (partner)
Physical practice
Models
Off-site trips
Role playing

Tactile:
Games
Highlighter pens
Post-it® notes/flags
Handouts
Notebooks/pens

Auditory:
Music
Singing
Video
Audiotape
Group discussion
Unusual sounds
Verbal review
Question sessions
Voice modulation

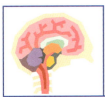

SENSORY and PERCEPTUAL LEARNING

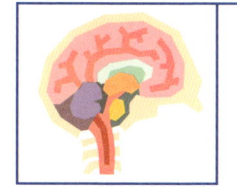

SENSORY and PERCEPTUAL LEARNING

VISUAL LEARNERS

45% of your clients or audience members want to **LOOK AT** something interesting while you are talking to them. Give them something to read or review such as brochures, handouts, PowerPoint, or flip charts. They literally can't hear you if there is nothing to look at!

◆ Post the results of your meeting on a storyboard, flip-chart or whiteboard outside the meeting room.

◆ Have posters about products, programs and other services posted in the meeting room.

◆ Review Chapter 6, Adding Visual Impact, for tips and techniques to capture your audience's visual attention.

VISUAL LEARNERS

If you have a visual learning style and are making a presentation or facilitating a meeting, make an effort to listen more intently to others. Keep your eyes focused on the other person when they are speaking to help avoid the appearance of being distracted or uninterested. Work on your listening skills. Practice speaking extemporaneously and try not to read verbatim from your notes.

Visual people will tend to forget the content of conversations and need to have written material to remind them of what was said. For them, distribute a written summary at the end of the meeting or send a follow-up memo/e-mail outlining the key points you want them to remember. Give participants or clients additional sources of information on your topic. They will use them and appreciate having the information.

SENSORY and PERCEPTUAL LEARNING

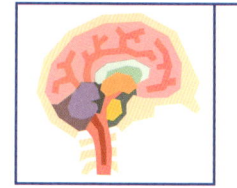

SENSORY *and* PERCEPTUAL LEARNING

VISUAL LEARNERS

Visual learners think and work best when able to see, visualize, read or review material in writing. They prefer to:

- draft or sketch their ideas out on paper, take notes
- read something - they will actually read the manuals, brochures and other written material you give them
- work/talk alone or in a quiet, uncluttered place - it cuts down on visual distractions
- look at you while you are speaking - they have a harder time with telephone and conference calls. They like e-mail and are easily distracted when on the phone

AVOID GIVING visual learners too much to look at in the beginning of your meeting or presentation. They will want to begin reading all the material right away. Give them written material a few pieces at a time as necessary during your session.

LANGUAGE CUES

You can mirror the vocabulary of your listener(s) to create greater rapport and increase the effectiveness of your communication.

VISUALS may use the following words/phrases when speaking or writing:
- Looking good!
- Get the picture?
- Look at it my way
- In my mind's eye
- Keep an eye out
- Seeing is believing

> **Visuals are not very animated with their body language and are usually quite contained.**
>
> **They may also speak in a more monotone voice.**

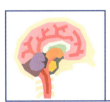

SENSORY and PERCEPTUAL LEARNING

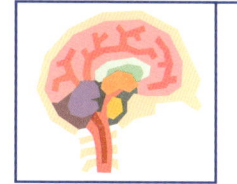

SENSORY and PERCEPTUAL LEARNING

KINESTHETIC LEARNERS

Kinesthetic learners need action! They are often problem-solvers and prefer quick, to-the-point conversations or information. They do not like to continue talking once a problem has been solved. They make up 20% of your audience, clients or employees.

◆   Ask them to volunteer to DO something during your presentation

◆   Use group exercises, dyad or team interactions

◆   Give them something to eat or drink and have frequent, 30-second stretch breaks

Kinesthetic individuals want to be able to move while they are thinking and may be considered blunt in their speech. They prefer to be short on words and long on action!

KINESTHETIC LEARNERS

If you have a kinesthetic style and are making a presentation or facilitating a meeting, you should focus on explaining yourself clearly and giving the other styles enough time to process and discuss your information.

Try to expend some energy before your presentation: exercise, take a walk or run up and down the stairs. This will make you calmer and more able to sit, stand or be in one place for a longer period of time and not be over-active in the front of the room.

Watch for over-use of hand gestures and standing too close to others (boundary invasion).

Work on incorporating the language of other styles into your communication. It will make the other styles feel more comfortable with what you have to say. Kinesthetic leaders should make an effort to explain their decisions before they take action, not after the fact.

SENSORY and PERCEPTUAL LEARNING

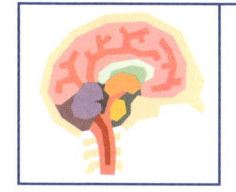

SENSORY and PERCEPTUAL LEARNING

KINESTHETIC LEARNERS

Kinesthetic learners think and work best when able to move and do things with their bodies. They prefer physical labor and communicating in person. They prefer to:

- stand, pace and move around while thinking, talking
- vary their activities - mix short tasks in with longer ones
- meet in person
- get on with the task at hand...they are action people!

AVOID GIVING kinesthetic learners too much information to read. They won't read it anyway and their manuals just gather dust on the shelf. They also have a limited amount of patience for meetings, or anywhere they have to sit still for too long. They much prefer to learn by doing it themselves, experimenting and figuring things out as they go along.

LANGUAGE CUES

You can mirror the vocabulary of your listener(s) to create greater rapport and increase the effectiveness of your communication.

KINESTHETICS may use the following words/phrases when speaking or writing:
- Let's jump on it!
- It's either sink or swim
- I can tackle that one
- I'm in for the ride
- We're getting closer
- Let's move!

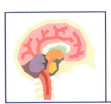

SENSORY and PERCEPTUAL LEARNING

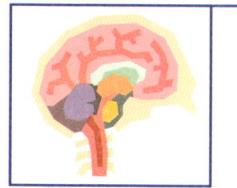

SENSORY and PERCEPTUAL LEARNING

TACTILE LEARNERS

20-25% of your clients or audience members want to **TOUCH** or handle something while you are talking to them. They are the fiddlers, doodlers and toe-tappers in your audience. Quite often, a visual learner's secondary style is tactile. What this means is that a *significant* number of people need something to touch AND look at when they are listening.

- Give them something to write on and write with. They will take lots of notes, even if they never go back and read them. The act of writing itself helps them process the information.

- Keep small objects such as mints, highlighters, Post-it® pads, pencils, etc. on the tables for them to use and touch. Keep a water pitcher and glasses on the table if possible.

TACTILE LEARNERS

Tactile learners, unlike kinesthetics who are whole-body movers, concentrate physical activity in their extremities; i.e. in their hands, head and feet.

If you have a tactile learning style and are making a presentation or facilitating a meeting, be aware that some of your habits may be distracting to your listeners. Avoid chewing gum, shuffling papers, putting your hands in your pockets, tapping your feet or touching your hair and face too often. As with the other styles, tactiles should work on incorporating the language of the other styles into their communication. Avoid your tendency to stand still, making sure to move your body as you speak. Avoid using a podium if possible.

Holding something in your hands while you talk can help you focus your attention on what you have to say. It will also attract the attention of the visuals in your audience.

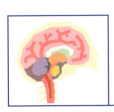

SENSORY and PERCEPTUAL LEARNING

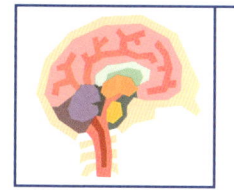

SENSORY and PERCEPTUAL LEARNING

28

TACTILE LEARNERS

Tactile learners think and work best when they can touch something and are able to use their extremities (hands, head, feet). Let them learn by doing. They like to:

- draft or sketch their ideas out on paper; taking notes helps them think
- have an opportunity to raise their hands, ask questions
- work with their hands
- decorate their work areas with small objects, desk toys, things they can touch

IF YOU ARE a tactile learner you need external stimulation in order to learn. You have terrific hand-eye coordination. When reading, highlight passages or key points.   Mints or gum may help you stay focused if you need to attend a long meeting or lecture.

LANGUAGE CUES

You can mirror the vocabulary of your listener(s) to create greater rapport and increase the effectiveness of your communication.

TACTILES may use the following words/phrases when speaking or writing:

- Feels good
- Hold on now!
- Get a grip
- Did you catch that?
- Hang in there
- Come to grips with it

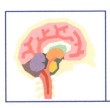

SENSORY and PERCEPTUAL LEARNING

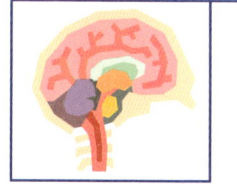

SENSORY and PERCEPTUAL LEARNING

AUDITORY LEARNERS

Only 10% of your employees, customers or audience members are auditory. What that means is that only one in 10 people really retain what they hear. Since they are remarkably good at remembering what they hear, but NOT what they see, auditories have their own unique learning challenges.

- They are NOT good "paper and pencil" test takers. Give them an opportunity to tell you what they have learned; they excel at oral tests and are much better with this format.

- They do not take notes, or read the manuals you give them. If they do read, they can remember the material better if they read out loud. Highlighting key points and phrases as they read also helps anchor the information in their brains.

AUDITORY LEARNERS

If you have an auditory learning style and are making a presentation or facilitating a meeting, you are fortunate as you probably have a natural ability for speaking in front of a group. However, focus on keeping your communication to the point, as you have a tendency to digress. You are a good listener. Mirroring the language style of your participants comes easily to you and you may find yourself mimicking their accents as well.

You are able to express yourself easily and naturally. As a result, you may unconsciously dominate a discussion or meeting. Make a point of not speaking for a few minutes to allow the others, particularly the visuals, an opportunity to talk.

Before making a presentation, repeat it a few times in your head or out loud to hear how it sounds.

SENSORY and PERCEPTUAL LEARNING

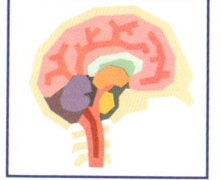

SENSORY and PERCEPTUAL LEARNING

AUDITORY LEARNERS

While auditory learners are natural speakers, they are also the best listeners. They think and work best when they can:

- think out loud or brainstorm verbally with others
- listen to books on tape, or have someone read to them. They very seldom read for pleasure
- "write" with a tape recorder
- communicate verbally; talk in person or on the phone - they dislike e-mail/memos

Call auditory participants on the phone for a brief "chat" *before* your meeting to help keep the meeting time down. When speaking with an auditory learner, vary the tone of your voice frequently. Mimic their enthusiasm and inflection.

LANGUAGE CUES

You can mirror the vocabulary of your listener(s) to create greater rapport and increase the effectiveness of your communication.

AUDITORIES may use the following words/phrases when speaking or writing:
- Sounds good
- Rings true
- Clear as a bell
- Face the music
- Lend me your ear
- Hear me out

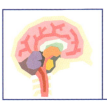

SENSORY and PERCEPTUAL LEARNING

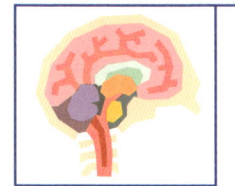

SENSORY and PERCEPTUAL LEARNING

LEARNING STYLES PRACTICE

Which styles would be more inclined to use the following statements?

_____ I've just been reviewing your proposal and it looks great!

_____ It sounds like a great deal, so let's talk about it.

_____ This is a beautiful piece of work.

_____ Is there something I can give you a hand with?

_____ We're not seeing eye to eye on this.

_____ Let's see how this flies with the rest of the team before we go any further.

_____ If you would listen to reason, you'd understand what I've been trying to say.

_____ I'll decide what I'm going to do and get back with you.

_____ Let me run this information by you again to make sure I understand it.

LEARNING STYLES PRACTICE cont.

_____	That feels good to me.
_____	I'll believe it when I see it!
_____	I can't seem to get a handle on it - could you show me?
_____	That's what I've been trying to tell you since the beginning.
_____	I'd like to move on our decision before the end of next week.
_____	If you can hold on a minute, I'll be right with you.
_____	That's music to my ears!

Remember to be perceptive, and listen for these cues when someone else is talking to you. Mirror their language, and they will remember what you have to say.

To take an online Learning Styles test, go to http://www.jackwolflearning.com/learning and click on the learning assessment tool.

SENSORY and PERCEPTUAL LEARNING

Our inherent style tells us much about how we express ourselves, communicate, and react to the actions of others. Discovering "who you are" and understanding how you can accommodate others who have different preferences and traits will help you present, communicate and interact more effectively.

Chapter 2 - Presentation Styles

Psychiatrist Carl Jung introduced the world to the theory of personality types back in the 1930s. In the years since, many others have developed their own interpretations of Dr. Jung's concepts, effectively tweaking them in various business and industry applications.

The communication perception that you leave after an interaction with your audience, whether it is one-on-one, as a group or in front of a whole room, is closely tied to your personality style. You also communicate your personality through written correspondence, e-mail, business cards, marketing material and other literature.

Speaking from "The Center of the Room"

First and foremost, you must discover who you are as a communicator. Get feedback from others and do a little research - there is much information available on the subject. Armed with your new knowledge, learn to be more flexible and react to the specific combination of personality traits in the person or group of people in front of you. Tone down (or ramp up!) your style to match theirs.

PRESENTATION STYLES

You can learn to recognize key personality traits in others simply by observing and listening. Do they ask questions, or simply tell you what they want you to do? Do they ask about your family or engage in small talk before getting down to the business at hand? A good way to get to know about others is to ask open-ended questions that will get them talking. You can observe many cues that will let you know who they are and, more importantly, what is important to them. For example, relationship-oriented people are concerned with how their actions (and the actions of the team, company, etc.) will affect others. Thinkers will base decisions on as much data as you can give them, while feelers let their instincts and intuition guide their decisions. Other individuals may want only the bottom line or have specific agendas and objectives.

Your goal is to engage each person in your audience during every interaction. Your audience can be as small as a single person or large enough to fill a ballroom and can range from peers, family members, co-workers and employees to potential customers or complete strangers. If you are speaking to a large group, you can achieve balance in your delivery style by speaking from the "center" of all of the styles.

Being neutral in presentation style does not mean being boring, it just means making sure to connect with the diversity in your audience. Set an agenda, ask for questions and feedback, base your information on facts, include a few personal stories or anecdotes, give clear outcomes and goals, and create safety and ownership in the room. If you can accomplish all this you will have discovered a sure-fire way to increase your effectiveness with your audience.

According to Jung, there are four primary personality trait dynamics. Individuals usually lean towards one trait in each of the four dynamic categories. These groups are: formal or informal, aggressive or easy-going, task or relationship-oriented, and thinkers or feelers. The various combinations of these eight characteristics create the templates for adult personalities.

Personal, outward communication traits are discernible once almost any interpersonal interaction begins.

PRESENTATION STYLES

PRESENTATION STYLES

In summary, to communicate effectively you must:

- Understand your own presentation style
- Receive feedback from others that verifies your beliefs about yourself
- Learn who your audience is - what are their personality types?
- Learn how to engage all styles when communicating

Four Primary Presentation/Personality Styles:

Controller: Aggressive, formal, thinker, task-oriented.
Asks: *What, When* - results-oriented questions

Promoter: Aggressive, informal, feeler, people-oriented.
Asks: *Who, When* - personal, dominant questions

Analyzer: Easy-going, formal, thinker, task-oriented.
Asks: *How-* technical, analytical questions

Supporter: Easy-going, informal, feeler, people-oriented.
Asks: *Who, Why* - personal, non-goal questions

Controller - Ready-Fire-Fire!

Controllers are born leaders and believe they can "do" it better than anyone else. They <u>may</u> listen to someone else's opinion if there is mutual respect (equal power or control). They have strong opinions and will hotly defend their point of view.

Controllers are rushed for time and value results. They will wing it sometimes without a lot of data. They want the "bottom line".

Acknowledge their results. They need you to tell them how good they are at getting the job done. If you want them to do something, give them a few options and let them control the decision. Watch for boredom and impatience.

- ▲ Strongest of styles
- ▲ Left-brain oriented
- ▲ Fast Thinker - last word
- ▲ "Not always right ... but never in doubt!"
- ▲ Good negotiators - political
- ▲ Results oriented, focused
- ▲ Get to the bottom line
- ▲ Don't push - they want to be in control of the decision
- ▲ President - Richard Nixon
- ▲ Task, teller, thinker, formal, aggressive

PRESENTATION STYLES

PRESENTATION STYLES

Promoter - Ready-Fire-Aim! (oops)

Promoters are the consummate creators. They like new and exciting projects and people; invigorating, stimulating and interactive environments.

Promoters are social, they need to be with people, talk and create. They follow their gut feeling rather than all of the data.

Acknowledge their creativity and people skills. They want to have some fun while creating results. Also, they may like to physically move when thinking or concentrating.

- ❖ Very social, craves personal interaction
- ❖ Hates routine, loves variety
- ❖ Creative; idea person; easily bored
- ❖ Lacks follow-through
- ❖ Thinks it and says it!
- ❖ Hates rules and regulations
- ❖ Most motivational
- ❖ Follows gut feelings, intuition
- ❖ High energy, scattered, unfocused
- ❖ President - Bill Clinton
- ❖ Relationship, teller, feeler, informal, aggressive

Supporter - Ready-Ready-Ready. . .

Supporters thrive on relationships and the approval of others.

The Supporter is the consummate team player. They will keep the peace. They are also the best listeners. They do not like confrontation. If pressured, they will agree ("Okay, I'll do it") and then withdraw for no apparent reason.

Remember to compliment who they are and what they do. Put Supporters on teams to help create a sense of belonging. Ask them the best way you can assist them in feeling safe. Because they like the feeling of being needed by everyone else, Supporters need to be careful not to get over committed.

- ❤ Doesn't like to be center of attention
- ❤ Non-judgemental, thinks of others
- ❤ Indecisive, avoids conflict
- ❤ Needs to be "needed"
- ❤ Works best on a team
- ❤ Motivated by deadlines
- ❤ Best listener, communicator
- ❤ Sensitive, empathic
- ❤ President - Jimmy Carter
- ❤ Relationship, asker, feeler, informal, easy-going

PRESENTATION STYLES

PRESENTATION STYLES

Analyzer - Ready-Aim-Aim. . .

Analyzers like to think before they take action. Give an Analyzer enough data and make an agreement with them on a decision time (by when). Be clear with what you want from them and when you want it. If you push an Analyzer to give an answer or take action too quickly, they will stall, request more information or simply withdraw.

They will want all of the details and historical data about your product or service in order to make an informed decision.

The Analyzer prefers to have multiple alternatives and reacts better to logical, well thought out plans with lots of options.

- Needs details to make decision
- Hesitant, most resistant to change
- Loves rules, manuals
- Gets the job done - but has difficulty delegating
- Collects information, organized
- Give them a "by-when" date
- Dislikes estimates, likes precision
- Sequential, logical thinker
- President - Gerald Ford
- Task, asker, thinker, formal, easy-going

At times, who you are the least (the style the most opposite from you) may be the most important style in your audience.

Manager (controller?) - Employee (supporter?)
Salesperson (promoter?) - Prospect (analyzer?)

PRESENTATION STYLES

Change your thinking and change your results.

Chapter 3 - Before You Begin

The following few pages deal with establishing a good environment for facilitating a meeting or delivering a training session. Many of the tips and techniques are also useful when meeting with someone one-on-one.

Before your meeting or presentation, your primary concerns should be:
- Knowing who your audience is
- What their skill or knowledge levels are
- What their expectations are
- HOW you are going to present your material to stimulate learning and retention:
  - What adult learning methods are you incorporating?
  - How can you address all of the potential learning styles in your audience?
  - What kind of room set-up promotes maximum learning and participation?

BEFORE YOU BEGIN

THE THEORY OF EXPECTANCY

Grade from 1 - 10 your belief about the future of your (or your company's) business success - what you really believe in your heart of hearts about your future. Done?

What would you say if I told you that this is more likely to happen...simply because you believe it will? The theory of expectancy states that your expectations unconsciously affect your behavior and, therefore, your outcomes. If your customer or audience expects a positive result from meeting with you, they are much more likely to perceive the experience that way.

- ◆ What can you do to help your customers/participants approach your meeting/training/ presentation session in a positive way? Give them reasons why they will benefit from attending.

    - ◆ Do you know what their beliefs are about you, your company, products, services or information? How can you overcome any negative attitudes/beliefs?

PRE-MEETING CONTACT

The week before your meeting, you can send your participants a short questionnaire to:

- Collect data about what your customer wants to achieve from the meeting
- Ask your customer what his or her knowledge level is on certain products/services
- Ask employees or team members what their priorities are
- Pre-test them on their current performance/results
- Ask your future participants what their current skill level/knowledge is and customize your presentation to their needs

Send your agenda and other learning points in advance to everyone. When possible, ask for their feedback about the agenda and be prepared to address any additional points during your meeting or presentation.

BEFORE YOU BEGIN

BEFORE YOU BEGIN

VOICE CHECK (how do you sound?)

Your voice is one of the most memorable things about you as a speaker. 37% of what your audience remembers about you and your presentation 30 days afterwards is your tone of voice, inflection, enthusiasm and your languaging (HOW you said your message which is different from remembering WHAT you said).

Most people are surprised to hear themselves as others do. Get a professional voice check, or ask someone whose feedback you respect to listen to your presentation. Tape record yourself and play it back with a critical ear to your tone, pacing and confidence. Do you pause unnecessarily or use filler words such as "um"? Describe your voice to yourself. If you had to sit in the audience with you as the speaker, would you want to?

**After 30 days, only 9% of what your audience will remember
is what you actually said.**

VISUAL CHECK (How do you look?)

What you look like and other visual aspects of your presentation make up a whopping 54% of what your audience will remember after your presentation. In addition to making sure your presentation is visually appealing, have someone whose opinion you value watch your presentation and give you a "visual report card".

Have someone videotape you in action. Get the audience on tape as well as yourself. Whether it is a live presentation or a rehearsal, you can get a clear idea of your visual impact on your audience. Get coaching on your "front of the room" skills from a professional if necessary.

Watch a video of another presenter you admire; watch presenters on television. Try to pinpoint what they are doing right. Hand gestures, stance, movement, dress and style are very important and convey another message behind the obvious one.

Things to avoid:
- Swaying or rocking from side to side
- Pointing to participants
- Turning your back to your audience
- Hiding behind the podium
- Not moving at all

BEFORE YOU BEGIN

BEFORE YOU BEGIN

ROOM SET-UP - Making it comfortable

Pay attention to your room set-up. Create a positive physical environment wherever learning is to take place. Small group seating, attractive surroundings, good lighting, stimulating visuals, etc. help create the optimum learning space. Here are a few check-points:

- Are the chairs comfortable?
- Is the lighting too harsh?
- Can the air conditioning/heating be adjusted during your session if necessary?
- Is it easy for participants to take notes and do interactive exercises?
- Is the space too big or too cramped for the size of your group?
    - Sit out where your audience will be. Would you want to spend an hour (or a day) sitting there?

ROOM SET-UP - Make it inviting and interesting to come in

- Have music or something visual to invite your participants into the room.
- Place something on the tables or chairs for the early birds to do while they are waiting to start. Put a puzzle up on an overhead. Copy brain teaser puzzles and put them on each table with pencils or pens.
- Have flip charts or post signs in the hallway to make it easy to find your session room.
- Post a rhetorical question on a flip chart for people to think about as they enter the room.
- Will you have something light to eat or drink? It will stimulate the senses and perk your audience up.

BEFORE YOU BEGIN

BEFORE YOU BEGIN

ROOM SET-UP - Creating the learning space

◆ Whenever possible, use round tables to seat 6-8 to allow for facilitation using a small group format. This will promote classroom safety and a feeling of intimacy in a large room. Place chairs in a crescent around the table so that everyone can face the speaker.

◆ Remove extra chairs once everyone has arrived.

◆ Can you tape or pin flip chart pages to the walls (storyboarding) as you go through your program? This technique will keep those ideas in your audience's mind as you move on to other points.

◆ Have something for your participants to write with and write on when they enter the room.

ROOM SET-UP - Audio-visual and equipment check

- Check the lighting fixtures, locations of switches, etc. before you begin.
- Place your main visual stimulator (projection screen, etc.) to the audience's FRONT LEFT if possible (front right if you are left-handed). If you place it in the middle of the room, you will have to compete with it the entire time, even when you are not using it.
- Keep a power strip with a long cord in your training bag. You never know when you'll need one.
- Have you had a sound-check if you are using a hand held microphone or lavaliere?
- Has the hotel or conference center assigned you a room that is next to something that will interfere with your presentation? A yoga seminar next door is one thing, but a reunion of trumpet players would be quite annoying. Find out who your neighbors are going to be.

BEFORE YOU BEGIN

BEFORE YOU BEGIN

PRESENTATION TOOL KIT

Before making your presentation (or facilitating a meeting), make certain you have all of the tools you need in advance to make it a success.

Here are some items to keep in your presentation tool kit. These items are for your participants to use and should be placed on the tables before your meeting starts:

- Colored, 3x5 index cards - see Chapter 7, Presentation Basics, for different techniques using 3x5 cards

- Small, colored dots or Post-it® flags for a different way to mark responses and note pages

- Pens with a highlighter on one end. Participants can take notes and highlight certain sections they want to return to later

  - Post-it® note pads - for collecting data, making notes, interactive exercises such as "What Questions"

PRESENTATION TOOL KIT

More ideas and things to include in your presentation tool kit. These items are for you to use:

- Small timer or clock - you need to keep track of the time, but keep it out of view of your audience. It is much better than looking at your watch every few minutes
- Marketing material – business cards
- Auditory "interrupts" such as a whistle, bell or chime. Guaranteed to quiet chatter and get their attention when you want to begin
- Small rewards for volunteers. Give them an incentive to come up to the front of the room!
- Colored, water-based flip-chart markers such as Mr. Sketch (won't bleed through paper)
- Supply of colored pens/markers for participants to make their name badges/tents

BEFORE YOU BEGIN

BEFORE YOU BEGIN

MORE POINTS TO CONSIDER

◆ Is this a new class/meeting or a continuation in a series?

◆ Do they know why they are attending? Is attendance voluntary or mandatory?

◆ Do the participants know each other? Are they meeting for the first time? Do they know you?

◆ Will your participants be distracted during your meeting? I.e. managers who have beepers, or need to check e-mail or phone messages frequently. Be supportive of their concerns.

◆ Are your participants novices, experts or a mix? Are they open to new ideas and information?

◆ What do they have to "unlearn" before they will change their beliefs/behavior? Many of your learners will have to unlearn what they've already learned in order to absorb and retain what it is you want them to know! Be considerate of their learn - unlearn - relearn dilemma.

Chapter 4 - Creating Safety & Ownership

Safety and ownership are two key ingredients to a successful presentation. When your audience is comfortable and relaxed they will feel safe enough to participate and will learn more. In addition, if they enter the room with the perception that they are going to have a good experience, they probably will.

Safety, in this context, is defined by the ability of your audience/client/listener to participate at their own pace and not at the request of the facilitator/speaker. If they have a belief that they will be called on, most participants will not be listening to whoever else is talking at the moment, but preparing in their own minds what they are going to say when it is their turn.

Ownership occurs when your client or audience feels that they have a stake in the outcome of the meeting or presentation. Flexibility, choice, contribution, equality and a belief that it matters that they are there all increase participation and learning.

SAFETY & OWNERSHIP = PARTICIPATION & LEARNING

CREATING SAFETY & OWNERSHIP

The word education comes from the Greek, "to make equal"

Increasing the perceived levels of equality in a learning session increases your participants' self-esteem and levels of participation.

By eliminating titles (aka declarations of seniority) on name badges and during introductions, lower-level employees will feel more comfortable when participating. In a diverse group, titles often raise anxiety about rocking the boat or saying something not in agreement with management during the session.

Let your participants sit wherever they choose in the room, or form their own small groups as they arrive. Give them the flexibility to select their dyad partners, particularly if they will be working with the same one extensively throughout the session.

SOCIALIZATION

To socialize your participants gently and to get them introduced to one another with as little stress as possible, start small, easing them into larger group interactions. Since personal feelings of risk increase as the group size gets larger, progress through the levels until your group/team is ready for a whole room exercise.

      Level 1. Individual assessment - get them writing or doing something by themselves at the very start

      Level 2. Dyad - one on one partner exercise (let them choose their partner)

      Level 3. Small group interaction (six people or less)

      Level 4. Whole room activity, icebreakers (recommended for the middle or end of your program)

CREATING SAFETY & OWNERSHIP

CREATING SAFETY & OWNERSHIP

WHAT BOARD PROCESS

Create a "What Board" for your training or meeting room. Before beginning, ask participants what their greatest challenge is day-to-day in their environment. Ask for their answers in writing (place small pads of Post-it® notes on each table or desk before beginning your session). Collect and post the responses on a whiteboard or flip chart in the front of the room.

Ask participants to select a partner and discuss their challenges with each other. This will get them to the next level of socialization and ready for action! Make sure each partner has equal time to speak.

As you progress through the meeting, presentation or workshop, address your audience's concerns and issues. Participants will come away from the session with a sense that their personal concerns are important to you, the company, etc.

ENCOURAGING QUESTIONS

Encourage questions from your audience. At the beginning of the meeting or presentation, establish a question and answer protocol. When someone asks a question, thank them for participating. If someone asks a question about something you just covered a few moments ago, answer it briefly without comment. You'll make others feel more at ease when they want to ask their own question.

Avoid calling on someone in your audience to answer a question or add their comments to the discussion if they have not asked to be recognized. This is a tension-raiser. That person may not have been paying attention, may not understand the question or they may be hesitant to give an opinion that is not in agreement with yours or management's.

Increase safety by asking participants to write their questions on 3x5 cards. Collect the cards right before each break and set aside a few minutes (or more) for discussion later during the session.

CREATING SAFETY & OWNERSHIP

CREATING SAFETY & OWNERSHIP

INTRODUCTIONS

Remember, 80% of us would rather *die* than present to a group of more than six people!

This also applies to getting up and being the center of attention in any large group. <u>You</u> may shine in the front of the room, but most of your audience members would most likely prefer to stay out of the spotlight.

Avoid the usual stand-up/sit-down round of introductions with name, title, etc. at the beginning of your presentation or meeting. Group introductions create anxiety. Many participants will be concerned and thinking about what they are going to say when it is their turn and are not listening to the other speakers anyway.

"GETTING TO KNOW YOU"

After some type of Level 1 individual assessment activity, continue your presentation with **partner or small table/group** introductions before you begin in earnest.

Ask participants to choose a partner or form small groups of 4-6 and give their name, where they were born, a unique experience, etc. Stay away from job titles and descriptions, etc. Keep it informal and light.

Name tents or badges promote ownership and a feeling of camaraderie. People appreciate it when you use their name when speaking directly to them during a presentation or meeting. As mentioned earlier in the chapter, eliminate titles from name badges and tents. Let participants make their own with a variety of colored markers available at their tables or as they come into the room.

CREATING SAFETY & OWNERSHIP

CREATING SAFETY & OWNERSHIP

WHEN IN DOUBT, WRITE IT OUT!

People are more attached to what they write than what they say. And people usually think about something a little harder before they write it down. Remember:

"People will not argue with their own data when it is in writing!"

To promote ownership of the data when asking for feedback, opinions or other subjective information, ask your participants to put their answers in writing. Their responses will be more accurate and less likely to be disputed later.

Post-it® notes should be standard equipment in your presentation tool kit. Short responses, once they are written down, can be passed forward to post on a flip chart or used as a discussion point in a dyad exercise.

LANGUAGE TIPS

- Be aware of using absolute language when presenting and speaking. Always and never should be used infrequently.

- Keep criticism to yourself (i.e. your competitors or their products, other clients). Negativity is contagious.

- Be cautious of using inappropriate or slang language. You may not know your audience as well as you think you do.

- Your audience will always appreciate being treated with respect. Terms such as "you guys", "you people" or "old folks" can be taken negatively by some individuals.

CREATING SAFETY & OWNERSHIP

CREATING SAFETY & OWNERSHIP

USING ICEBREAKERS

Use an icebreaker to acquaint people with each other beyond the initial introductions. Whole-group icebreakers do not belong in the beginning of your session unless the attendees already know each other. Since a whole-group icebreaker falls into level 4 of socialization, it should be incorporated into the middle of your program after everyone has had an opportunity to get more comfortable. Make sure the icebreaker is light, fun and does not invade the boundaries of the participants by asking uncomfortable personal questions or requiring physical contact.

For a fun icebreaker break, ask everyone to share what their very first job was and the best/worst moment they had at that job. Afterwards, the group declares who gets a prize for the best/worst. This is a great way to make everyone aware that their co-workers' lives did not start on the day they came to work at the company.

ICEBREAKER BENEFITS

- To get people better acquainted
- To alleviate stress, or liven up a long stretch of technical information
- To refocus your team/group after the lunch break
- To get people more comfortable
- To get the audience moving and participating
- As a review of the information covered up to that point in the session
- To establish a community-like feeling among participants; team building
- Just for fun!

CREATING SAFETY & OWNERSHIP

CREATING SAFETY & OWNERSHIP

TENSION

During a meeting, there may be periods of tension or high-stress. Anticipate them and be prepared with a few tactics to get through these moments.

Tension may occur:
- at the beginning of a meeting
- before a test, or question and answer period where participation is necessary
- when change is being discussed or implemented (i.e. behavior, performance, results)
- when giving negative feedback or discussing poor performance

If tension is high:

- begin a small group or partner exercise
- ask participants to write their top three concerns about the issue and discuss them with a partner or in small groups
- take a short stretch break; it sends oxygen to the brain and relaxes the body
- incorporate some humor (don't, however, rattle off a joke that has nothing to do with the situation)
- have your audience move or do something physical
- buffer negative statements with positive ones

CREATING SAFETY & OWNERSHIP

CREATING SAFETY & OWNERSHIP

BOUNDARIES

Boundaries are extremely important in small group and one-on-one interactions. Respect the boundaries of others, watch for their body language reactions to you, such as how they shake hands, how close they stand when in conversation or their facial and physical cues when interacting.

Mirror their boundaries. If they move back a step or two when talking to you, do not close the gap by moving closer. An individual's boundary can vary according to the situation or environment. Most people have distinct, and different, professional and personal boundaries - be aware of both.

POWER POSITIONS

When talking to others, try to stay at eye level and out of a power position, such as standing over someone who is seated.

If you are facilitating a meeting, try to position yourself democratically. Move your chair away from the head of the table or behind a desk. Position yourself to show that you are on equal ground. You will encourage increased participation in your meetings and a feeling that you are all in this together.

Any perception you may have of losing control or power is exactly that - your perception.

CREATING SAFETY & OWNERSHIP

CREATING SAFETY & OWNERSHIP

ROOM SET-UP RELATED TO SAFETY & PARTICIPATION

Room set-up is an important aspect of safety and participation. Horseshoe or "U" shaped arrangements expose participants face-to-face to the whole group. These create an environment that may be intimidating or unsafe for many participants. Try to avoid them if possible.

Room set-ups that use round tables to seat 6-8 are preferred and facilitate partner and small group exercises. Avoid overcrowding tables. People need space to spread out and move around once in a while. Have empty chairs removed or combine the people seated at half-empty tables.

When you can, provide chairs with wheels for the kinesthetic learner.

 In general, an inviting room that is the right size for the group, is comfortable, has proper lighting and temperature controls will contribute to higher levels of participation and learning. Look for more information on room set-up in Chapter 3, Before You Begin.

MORE TIPS TO CREATE SAFETY and OWNERSHIP

Ask for volunteers to help in the delivery by writing on flip charts or being small group or table leaders.

As frequently as possible, change the leadership of dyad and small group exercises. Assign new leaders by asking who has the longest/shortest tenure with company, largest/smallest car/shoe size, etc. It creates fun and rotates authority at the tables.

During breaks and lunch/dinner times have a group leader for each table help get everybody back on time (to choose leader: last person to stand, person with the most televisions at home, etc.)

Periodically rotate the participants to different tables if you can. It increases networking and helps to move difficult participants away from their support base.

CREATING SAFETY & OWNERSHIP

CREATING SAFETY & OWNERSHIP

How often do you travel that 15 inch road between your head and your heart as a presenter? Let your audience get to know you.

Your audience is as important as the material you are delivering. Acknowledge them and thank them for coming. No one appreciates a stand-offish expert. Share your knowledge and experiences with your audience with friendliness, passion and conviction.

Create a personal connection with your audience, team or client. Arrive before the appointed starting time, chat with early arrivals, don't disappear during the break and, in general, make yourself available.

If you ARE what you say and do, it shows - and your audience (client) will know it.

Chapter 5 - Handouts

Handouts and other printed materials are a very important part of any presentation you make. Like any first impression, your handouts, job-aids, brochures, etc. say a great deal about you, your organization and your services or products. Your materials set the tone of the meeting or presentation. Is it going to be informal or formal, technical, exciting or just plain old business as usual?

If you are designing your own material, you have a great opportunity to make sure your audience or customer remembers the information you want them to. The first phase of learning is always the arousal of interest. Does your material get them excited? Does it get them thinking? Does it stand out? Afterwards, what are you leaving behind? Have you made it worth keeping?

This chapter is based on adult learning and marketing research principles and includes basic (and some not so basic) information that will give you the ability to create top-notch, professional material your readers, audience and customers will remember.

HANDOUTS

WHY USE HANDOUTS

Every presentation or meeting (by phone or in person) with an audience or client should have a handout.

- It gives them a "track"
- It gives them something to refer back to
- It puts everything in writing
- It gives your visual learners something to look at
- It gives your tactile learners something to touch

What do your clients (audience) get to look at and touch while they are listening to you talk? Handouts will stimulate their brain and increase retention.

STIMULATE BOTH SIDES OF THEIR BRAIN!

When creating written material, use plenty of icons, visuals, and graphics to complement the words and numbers. They will stimulate the right-brain of your reader while the facts and figures will appeal to the left-brain. Touch, color, visual shifts and choice all play a role in creating interest in your printed material.

RIGHT BRAIN - VISUALS - tied to EMOTIONS
LEFT BRAIN - WORDS AND NUMBERS - tied to LOGIC

Make your handouts interactive - create fill-in-the-blanks, information boxes and leave additional space for notes. It will keep their attention on the page (and on what you are talking about) longer and keep them AWAKE!

HANDOUTS

A PICTURE REALLY IS WORTH A THOUSAND WORDS!

Are you aware that you have only 8-12 seconds to get your reader's visual attention? It is important that you incorporate something visual that gets your reader's attention immediately.

Your reader's eye is instinctively drawn to pictures first. Using pictures is an effective way to draw attention to text-heavy sections of your page and get them interested in reading.

Avoid using clip art that is too juvenile (which unfortunately includes much of what is available for free).

Your graphics help establish the level of professionalism in your handouts, brochures, etc.

MAKE YOUR HANDOUTS LOOK AS PROFESSIONAL AS POSSIBLE

A good design rule of thumb: Just because you can, doesn't mean you should. Too much of a good thing can be visually distracting.

- Keep your layout simple
- Use white space generously, leaving plenty of room for note-taking
- Number your pages for easy reference
- Find a layout you like and stick to it. Get ideas from other material you have seen. If you don't trust your own judgement, get someone else's opinion
- Be consistent with your format, colors, borders and page frames throughout your document. Use variations on a theme to create variety. Keep your colors in the same tonal family (you wouldn't wear pink socks with red pants would you?)

HANDOUTS

1/3 - 1/3 - 1/3

Every page of your handout or brochure contains three distinct sections. When designing your material, remember that the:

- top $1/3$ is the MOST read part of the page
- middle $1/3$ is the LEAST read part of the page
- bottom $1/3$ is the SECOND MOST read part of the page

Grab your readers' attention with the first line. Here is where you can make your point, create curiosity, or let them know why they should continue to read on.

EYE SWEEP

With single-page material, your readers' eyes will "sweep" the page from top left to bottom right. The area of the page with the most impact is the upper left. The lower left is considered a dead spot - use it for your least important information.

When material is double-sided and bound, or included in a publication such as a magazine or newspaper, the "page turning effect" makes the upper right corner of the right page the most visible section.

1/3 - 1/3 - 1/3

Use **graphics**, **colors**, **bulleted lists** and **text boxes** to draw attention (and gain retention) to the information in the middle of the page. Incorporate **shading** or **colored text** for extra visual interest. Make it distinctive! Another way to make the middle 1/3 of your brochure or handout page (the least read part of any page) stand out is to make it **interactive**:

- Use fill-in-the-blank sections
- Insert a colored graph
- Leave space (lined or unlined) on the page to take notes
- Ask your audience to highlight a word or phrase that is important
- Insert a pop quiz or "Did You Know" question box and let them fill in the answers

The lower right creates very high retention as it is the last part of a page that the eye scans. It is a good spot for your logo and other important information.

HANDOUTS

HANDOUTS

THE THEORY OF EYE CONTAINMENT (or... FRAME YOUR STUFF!)

Framed pages have a "contained" look that encourages the reader's eyes to stay focused longer on the material inside. So...

> Use frames or borders on your pages to draw the reader's eye. Framing important sections of text will draw attention to that area of the page. Keeping the frame format consistent avoids visual overload.

A subject-specific frame around your text adds visual interest and lets the reader know about the topic at a glance. Avoid using "cutesy" borders for professional material.

Using a combination of text frames (shaded and unshaded), clip art, photos and other graphics is an effective layout strategy that can be accomplished even when using the most common word processing software.

MAKE YOUR HANDOUTS EASY TO READ

- Use:
    - No more than 2 font styles on each page
    - All capitals for titles only
    - Sans serif type for short blocks of text*
    - Serif type for paragraphs or when using a condensed font style*
    - A larger point size than normal. (Your clients who need glasses may not be wearing them!)
- If stapling your handout, make it single-sided.
- If you are binding the material into booklets, print a border or frame around the edge of the reverse side of each page and a header with the word NOTES at the top. This will encourage participants to take notes.

> Serif
>
> Sans Serif

* The serif is the small stroke that crosses the main line of a letter. Sans serif fonts do not have this extra line. The serif actually helps draw your readers' eyes from one word to the next making it more suitable for paragraphs and whole pages of text.

HANDOUTS

USING THE RIGHT COLORS

Use soft colors (light blue, gray, tan, peach, rose, almond) when selecting your paper for hand-outs. Lightly colored paper is:

- easier on the reader's eye
- different
- remembered longer
- easier to find if it gets placed with other papers

These colors are also best for stationary, business cards and other material.

Using blues and greens as background colors creates a professional mood whereas the use of reds and yellows as highlights creates excitement and urgency.

 **White paper and black ink causes the greatest level of eye fatigue**

WHY USE COLOR

According to research by 3M, Kodak, Xerox and Hewlitt Packard, using color in your printed material increases:

- motivation and participation by 80%
- readership by 40%
- retention of the material by 18%
- response rates by 20%

So...be sure to use colored paper, ink and/or graphics, pictures and icons whenever possible.

HANDOUTS

WHERE TO USE COLOR

- Use a different colored paper for key pages in your handouts such as action plans, speaker's biography, reference and resource information and/or reviews and assessments.

- If your handout has more than one section, place a different colored "separator page" between them. Use a different color for the cover page.

- Avoid using fluorescent or very brightly colored paper.

- Colored text, headlines or titles can also be used to set specific information apart from the rest of the page. Using colored ink increases overall retention of printed material.

    - Try using colored text or colored bullets next to important points.

BEST IDEAS

BOX. Every 3 or 4 pages, box off a section of the page for best ideas. Ask your clients to write down their best ideas or what they need to remember. Give them Post-it® flags to mark the most important pages. They will go back to these pages often as a reference once the meeting is over.

PAGE. Dedicate one page as a "Best Ideas" page. Ask your participants (clients) to fill in their best ideas from the presentation periodically throughout your session. Make your Best Ideas page a **different color** for easy reference after the session.

Ask them to write down what they can (want to) act on now, later or items that require a decision. Ask them to write down the action steps that are necessary to implement their best ideas.

HANDOUTS

USING AN AGENDA

A lot of clients/learners want the facts - the bottom line. For them, set a written agenda. Incorporating a welcome letter and/or agenda page into the beginning of your handout can:

- set the tone for the meeting or presentation
- thank any sponsoring organization
- add a professional look to the material
- give your participants an overview of the topics
- outline goals and objectives
- thank them for attending

DISTRIBUTING YOUR MATERIALS

- Give your audience and clients handouts, brochures, marketing material and other information one piece at a time or as they need it. If you give them too much in the beginning, they may feel overwhelmed.

- You also run the risk of losing their attention once you hand out your materials. The visual learners in your audience will want to read the pages rather than listen to you talk and the tactile learners will be too busy flipping pages to pay attention.

- By giving materials out one piece at a time you focus their attention on what you want to discuss right now and keep control over the sequence of topics.

 HANDOUTS

HANDOUTS

CREATING A JARGON PAGE

Not everyone will be familiar with the industry-specific terms that you might use. To help your audience/client feel more comfortable with the jargon:

- Create a "jargon page" and place it near the back of your handout.

- Have them mark the word or phrase with a Post-it® flag.

- During your meeting or presentation, when you arrive at industry-specific words that may be unfamiliar to your clients or audience, discuss their meanings and ask them to write the words and the definitions on the jargon page. This is a useful reference for after the session.

  - Writing the words and definitions helps anchor the information in their long-term memory.

IMPLEMENTATION PAGE

Make one of the final pages of your handout an implementation page.

- "What" action is to be taken?
- "By when" is the action to be taken?
- "Who" is responsible for this action?
- "How" will the follow-up occur?

This "Action Plan" page can include business outcomes, personal goals, behavior changes and a list of people who can help your participants achieve them.

Include a column to compare their "Up to Now" results with their "From Now On" goals.

Creating Your Future........

PROFESSIONAL ACTION PLAN

The outcomes I want to create in my career/life are:

My "By When" Date:

What ACTION STEPS can I take with me today?

Who else do I need to network with in order to accomplish these steps?

My personal Board of Directors who can/will support me:

93

HANDOUTS

MARKETING

If you are an outside vendor, presenter or consultant, your handouts should be designed with future marketing in mind.

Be sure to include all of your contact information on the cover. You should include your name, address, phone number, e-mail and website.

Include a list of clients, credentials and expertise in your biography. This biography should be on the **last** page of your handout. If possible, make your bio specific to the interests of the client you are presenting to or their industry.

RESOURCES/REFERENCES

For your left-brained clients and audience members...

If you have additional technical or background information that you believe is necessary to incorporate somewhere, place it on several "read-only" pages in the back of the handout.

Instruct your participants to go back to these pages later for reference without taking a lot of time going over the details in the middle of your presentation. Those who want the information will be glad it is there.

Include any references to sources from which you have gathered information that might be of interest. Resist the temptation to load up on obscure references that no one will bother to look up anyway.

INCLUDE:
- **Books**
- **Tapes**
- **Videos**
- **Articles**
- **Web sites**
- **Conferences**

 HANDOUTS

Your audience would rather look at

than read the word

TREE

WHY?
**Because our minds think in visual images
rather than in words or numbers.**

Chapter 6 - Adding Visual Impact

By now, you understand the importance of stimulating the five senses, appealing to different learning and personality styles and of giving your participants something to touch and do. Even so, a visually stimulating presentation can often mean the difference between "ho-hum, so what" and "wow!"

VISUAL ATTENTION

You may know that you have only 8-12 seconds to get your audience's attention, but do you know that you only have 30-45 seconds to keep it? So...it's not enough to just get their attention when you start your presentation - you need to be constantly aware of re-engaging it!

One way to accomplish this is to give your audience (whoever they are....) a visual break. A visual break does not mean you ask your audience to close their eyes....it usually happens unconsciously with the blink of their eye. When you periodically refocus their attention, shifting their eyes to something new, you will be able to keep their attention much longer.

If it's worth saying, it's worth seeing!

ADDING VISUAL IMPACT

CREATING A VISUAL BREAK

Eyes are drawn to color and movement, so...

- Move frequently, stride across the room or simply snap your fingers
- Use hand and facial gestures
- Hold something colorful in your hands to attract attention (i.e. flip chart marker)
- Write on your flip chart in bold colors (avoiding red and yellows except to highlight)
- Hang a colorful banner on the wall
- Be colorful with your handouts - use pictures, icons and graphics
- Use a laser pointer to briefly highlight something on the projection screen

There are many ways to catch the eye. See how creative you can be!

MULTIPLE VISUAL STIMULATORS

You are at your least effective when only speaking to your audience - the spoken word is a very low level brain stimulator. To increase your impact when talking, whether it's to a small group, one-on-one, or in front of a large room, use multiple visual stimulators by using a variety of techniques to get your audience's (or client's) visual attention.

In addition to handouts and other printed material, use PowerPoint, overheads, storyboarding and flip charts.

Don't forget - YOU are a visual stimulator! Wear bold (but not too flamboyant) colors such as royal blue or dark red. A bright color on your tie or blouse will stimulate attention and, therefore, greater retention of what you are presenting.

ADDING VISUAL IMPACT

ADDING VISUAL IMPACT

POWERPOINT TIPS

Use PowerPoint or another visual presentation program if possible. This will add variety to your presentation while adding another level of professionalism. A cordless mouse will allow you to move around the room and not tie you to your laptop.

Let your PowerPoint (or overhead) act only as visual punctuation. Reading from the screen is a sure giveaway that you are not familiar with your material. Your focus should be on your audience rather than the screen, allowing you to make eye contact with participants and to gauge their reaction/interest immediately.

PROJECTION SCREEN

For larger audiences, have a projection screen available. The screen should not be placed center stage as this will take attention away from the rest of your presentation when it is not in use. Place the screen to one side, either on your audience's left if you are right-handed or to their right side if you are left-handed.

POWERPOINT TIPS

- Use movement and graphics, but do not overload your viewer's visual senses as it will detract from your message. Keep it visually engaging but CLEAR!

- Using a mix of both text and visuals in your presentation will ensure retention in both sides of the brain!

- Be wary of clip art that looks too juvenile - use high grade illustrations and photos wherever possible.

- When designing your PowerPoint presentation, roll your bulleted points up from the bottom so that the most important one ends up on top of the list.

- Remember the law of primacy and recency. Your audience will remember the first and last items on your list (if it contains more than three items). All the rest will soon be forgotten.

ADDING VISUAL IMPACT

ADDING VISUAL IMPACT

POWERPOINT TIPS

- Coordinate colors, templates and the overall look of each slide or slide series so that any combination appears to be a seamless, professional presentation.

- Avoid the use of dark text on medium backgrounds (such as blue) as it may not be visible on a large screen or if the room is not completely dark.

- Use a variety of points of entry but keep object and text transition types similar throughout. Choose a few you like and stick to them.

- Remember "eye sweep" from the chapter on handouts? The same holds true when designing your PowerPoints and overheads. The viewer's eyes will "sweep" the screen from top left to lower right. The area of the screen with the most impact is the upper left - put your logo here and other important information you want them to remember.

POWERPOINT TIPS

- Cover a single point or idea on each slide
- Choose your words carefully - avoid too much jargon
- Limit your sentence length and punctuation
- Use bulleted lists for a stronger impact (numbered lists imply priority - if all items have the same significance, use standard bullets rather than numbers)
- Use all capitals only for titles
- Use highlighting and revelation*
- Use but don't overuse color

> * **Zerconic Effect: If something is incomplete or only partially visible, we will pay more attention to it**

ADDING VISUAL IMPACT

ADDING VISUAL IMPACT

STORYBOARDING

Use a flip chart to "storyboard" your presentation. Tear off the pages from the flip chart and post them on the walls as you progress through your meeting or presentation. It will help your audience and clients remember your key points.

Also, if you want to go back to a point you've already made, this eliminates the headache of flipping backwards through the flip chart to find the page you want.

To quickly and easily storyboard pages from a flip chart, tear off 3" strips of masking tape and make tape rolls before the start of your session. Place the rolls on the back of the flip chart easel or on the edge of a table out of sight but easily reachable. When you need to post a page, simply grab a few pre-made tape rolls and stick them to the back of the paper. More expensive, but even easier, is using Post-it® flip chart paper.

FLIP CHARTS

Flip charts are an important component of almost any presentation. They can be put to very good use in a number of situations.

CHOOSING YOUR MARKERS

- Use water-based markers designed for flip charts such as Mr. Sketch. They won't bleed through to the next sheet and the smell is much milder than the chemical-based ones; some are even fruit-scented. (Much nicer!)
- Use broad-tipped, dark-colored markers. Reds, yellows and oranges are for highlighting only. Use dark colors such as black, brown, blue, purple and green when writing.
- Use two different colors on the same page, such as purple and dark green for contrast between topics, questions and answers, when making columns, or just to spice up the page.

ADDING VISUAL IMPACT

ADDING VISUAL IMPACT

USING FLIP CHARTS

- Frame the page or important information
- Brush up on your drawing skills - you don't have to be Picasso to make it interesting
- Make sure it's readable from the back of the room - print LARGE AND LEGIBLY!
- Stand to one side while writing - your participants will appreciate being able to see as you write
- Place a flip chart in the hallway to let them know they are in the right room
- Post a question to get them thinking about your topic before you start. "What if...?"
  - Create a "welcome page" for participants to look at as they come into the room
  - Post the session agenda or the desired outcomes of the meeting

Chapter 7 - Presentation Basics

Sometimes knowing where to begin can be a challenge. If you have been able to pre-assess your audience, you will be better prepared to deliver information geared specifically towards their needs and concerns. If you are opening with a limited amount of information about them, then there are a few assumptions that you should make. You should assume that:

- Your learners will encompass a variety of learning styles
- They may NOT be motivated or ready to learn
- They will have "real world" issues to address
- They will want to know how they can apply this knowledge in THEIR lives, both personally and professionally
- Just because they receive information does not mean that they will learn or use it

It is your job to ensure that learning does occur, and ultimately, behavior changed or action taken. The adult learning methods and techniques included in this chapter are designed to help you make your meeting/presentation/training a success.

PRESENTATION BASICS

WHERE IS YOUR FOCUS AS A PRESENTER?

As you increase your skill as a presenter, you will shift naturally from Level 1 to Level 4. Assess your current skill as a presenter. Are you focused on...

Level 1 - Presenter (YOU!): At level 1, you are primarily concerned with how you are received by your audience and their opinion of you. Your interaction with the audience is limited and you are more comfortable presenting from the power position of the room (head of the table, behind a podium, etc.) You may be new at presenting and feel nervous and uncomfortable.

Level 2 - Content: This level involves the simple delivery of information or the "what" of the presentation. You may lecture without any other visual or physical stimulation except a few flip charts or overheads. Once you deliver your information, any learning and application is left up to your recipient. When a presenter's focus is at Level 2, it is often because he or she is a subject matter expert but inexperienced as a presenter.

Level 3 - Audience: This is the first level of presentation to be outwardly focused on gaining and retaining an audience's attention. You know it is important for your audience not to be distracted by external issues and/or work pressures. You use a variety of delivery techniques, accommodate your participants' work related issues, and understand how accelerated learning principles and adult learning theory increases retention.

Level 4 - Learning: Congratulations! You are presenting at the highest level of effectiveness. In addition to level 3, your focus is on application, behavior change and increased performance. You incorporate post-learning tools and techniques such as job-aids, training follow-up, mentoring and/or coaching programs to reinforce learning and achieve the results that triggered the training in the first place.

Basic Principles of Adult Learning:

- Involve learners in planning and implementing learning activities
- Draw upon the learners' experiences
- Cultivate self-direction in learners
- Create a climate that encourages and supports learning
- Foster a spirit of collaboration
- Use small groups

Source: ERIC "Practice in Brief: Using Adult Learning Principles in Adult Basic and Literacy Education," 1998 Susan Imel.

PRESENTATION BASICS

PRESENTATION BASICS

"5 LEVELS OF ENGAGEMENT"

According to Bernard Shaw, "The greatest problem with communication is the illusion that it has been accomplished!" When you are presenting to and speaking with others (and it could be your audience, customer, spouse, children, employees, etc.), how do you know if you have their attention?

The worst assumption you can make when speaking is that the other person is listening!

What are you doing to get (and keep) your listener's attention?

LEVEL 1

When opening a meeting or presentation, you can break your listeners' preoccupation and get them engaged in your session by getting <u>them</u> to **TALK**:

- Have them repeat key information out loud
- Ask them questions
- Ask them for their questions
- Have them introduce themselves
- Ask them what they would like to learn from this meeting/presentation/etc.

PRESENTATION BASICS

"5 LEVELS OF ENGAGEMENT"

LEVEL 2

When opening a meeting or presentation you can break your listeners' preoccupation and get them engaged in your session by getting <u>them</u> to **MOVE**:

- ◆ Pass out handouts (another good reason to NOT hand them out ahead of time!)
- ◆ Get them writing – ask them to take notes
- ◆ Raising their hands to ask questions

LEVEL 3

Combines Levels 1 and 2 - If they are asking **UNSOLICITED QUESTIONS**, talking and moving, you really have their attention. This is self-paced public speaking!

LEVEL 4

Getting participants to **TAKE NOTES** engages their attention, keeps them moving and anchors the information visually and tactually. Do you know the difference between note-taking and note-making?

Note-taking involves writing down spoken material. But when participants start writing down their own notes and ideas (note-making), you'll know you've really gotten them thinking!

LEVEL 5

TEACHING OTHERS WHAT THEY'VE JUST LEARNED. If they can teach it/tell it/demonstrate it to others, you've accomplished your task.

PRESENTATION BASICS

RETENTION LEVELS

Results from a number of studies have all indicated the same thing. People remember something better if they can do it themselves or use the information fairly soon after they've learned it.

Mixing it up is the key. Presentations which include a variety of methods will achieve the best results. One of my favorite sayings is, *"Tell them, show them, let them."* This means that once you've told them, model or show examples of what you want to communicate and then, finally, let them practice using the information in ways that are relevant to their own lives and situations.

**INVOLVEMENT increases retention.
"The more I do, the more I remember."**

Actual retention levels for the different types of learning delivery and activities are:

Teaching others/immediate use 80%
Practice by doing............................75%
Discussion group....................50%
Demonstration...............30%
Audio-visual............20%
Reading.........10%
Lecture....5%

Retention of any information is based upon how it is received and processed. The higher the level of participation, both verbally and physically, the greater the retention of the material.

PRESENTATION BASICS

Courtesy of NTL Institute for Applied Behavioural Sciences

PRESENTATION BASICS

BRAIN BREAKS

Here's the good news: your listeners can pay attention for 45 minutes. Here's the bad news: they can pay attention WITH RETENTION for only 8-12 minutes before they take a brain break.

What's a brain break? Brain breaks are split second changes of focus. It's when your brain decides it's had enough new information delivered for now and makes a beeline for an unrelated thought or memory, such as what you are going to have for lunch once the meeting is over. During this brain break your brain files away the new pieces of information it has received. Unfortunately, once someone goes into brain break mode, it is not so easy to get their attention back.

> *Using accelerated learning techniques can help guarantee that as much of the material as possible will be learned and applied by your participants.*

Rather than fighting natural brain break tendencies, plan your presentation to stimulate them, both yours and your audiences'. Give your audience a deliberate brain break every 8-12 minutes to revive attention and boost retention. These split second changes of pace and focus are all it takes to get and keep your audience's attention from wandering off on its own.

BRAIN BREAKS TECHNIQUES

- get them writing, taking notes
- distribute handouts
- play music
- use visual props
- ask them to repeat something
- get them to reach for something
- get them to move their chair
- stand on your chair!
- get them to laugh
- give them something to drink/eat
- get them to talk - initiate a dyad or small group interaction
- shift their visual attention with PowerPoint, overheads, a flip chart, etc.

PRESENTATION BASICS

PRESENTATION BASICS

AUTO-PILOT

Our auto-pilots include things such as our beliefs about our learning and skills, the influence past experiences have on our present actions, cultural beliefs and attitudes, how we perceive ourselves and others and, finally, how we react to the world around us.

Our auto-pilots are in control 94.7% of the time. (yes, this is accurate)

When we wake every morning, we actually dress ourselves in our auto-pilot behaviors, attitudes and beliefs before we head out into our daily lives. Many of these auto-pilots are beneficial to us (like driving on the right side of the road). Many are not. How can we determine which are which? Some considerations for you as a presenter/facilitator are:

▶ What presentation auto-pilot habits do you need to unlearn to become a better presenter?

▶ How can your audience unlearn or change their habits to create different results?

POWERFUL WORDS

According to a study conducted by the Yale University English Department, the 12 most powerful words in the English language are:

- YOU
- SAVE
- EASY
- GUARANTEE
- MONEY
- RESULTS
- LOVE
- PROVEN
- DISCOVERY
- HEALTH
- NEW
- FREE

Of these, the word **YOU** has the most impact on your client, helping close more deals than any other. Your audience or client really wants to know what you have to offer means to him or her. Using the words I, we, my, mine and ours tells them that you are primarily focused on yourself and NOT on them. Aim for a ratio of 8 "you"s for every single "I, me, our, we, my, mine, us" you use in your conversations or written correspondence.

PRESENTATION BASICS

PRESENTATION BASICS

PRESENTATION TIPS

- Use the whole room when you present. Movement conveys energy and excitement.

- Make eye contact with your audience.

- Smile occasionally during your presentation. It shows you are in control and confident.

- Humor brightens any session and creates a sense of fun. It stimulates the brain and relaxes the mind.

- Build some suspense into your session. Hint at something in the beginning and reveal it later. Create curiosity - get them to ask!

-

PRESENTATION TIPS

- Stop your presentation midway through and ask participants to find a partner and explain what they have learned so far as if the other person had been out of the room.

- Tease your audience or listener with trivia questions. Little known but interesting facts about your topic can make it come alive.

- Incorporate interactive discovery exercises into your sessions. They can be personal, partnered or team-based.

- Your role as a presenter is to get your participants to think and talk about your ideas and to give them ways to integrate the material into their own lives. Give your audience practical and personal ways to implement the new information.

PRESENTATION BASICS

PRESENTATION BASICS

MORE PRESENTATION TIPS

◆ Have note paper/pads and pens available (imprinted, of course, with your company name). Your participants (clients) may not come prepared to learn.

◆ Be different - distribute colored pens to take notes with during your meeting. Colored printing increases retention and will make taking notes interesting.

◆ Remember, avoid white paper and black ink whenever possible.

◆ Keep business cards and small brochures available for those who ask.

◆ Give away items such as pens, note pads, triple-highlighter markers, etc. imprinted with your company name and contact information during and after your session.

MORE PRESENTATION TIPS

- It's all about being CLEAR. Tell your audience what you are going to tell them....then tell them....and finally, tell them what you just told them!

- Use metaphors when delivering your material to an audience - it will help your audience anchor a new concept in everyday terms.

- To improve attention give your learners a brain break by asking them to watch their hands as they move their right and left hands in figure-eight circles.

- "Don't think about pink elephants." Hard not to now, isn't it? Avoid the words not and don't in both spoken and written words. Say what you DO want rather than what you don't. It is hard for the brain to incorporate the negative into memory.

PRESENTATION BASICS

PRESENTATION BASICS

RULE OF THREE
Your audience will remember information better if it is delivered in chunks of three. Whenever possible, roll out your information in groups of three ideas/concepts rather than in one long list.

PRIMACY AND RECENCY
When presenting information, people will remember the first (primacy) and last (recency) items they hear or see. Arrange bulleted lists with the most important items first and last when designing PowerPoint slides as well as written material.

FIVE KEY POINTS
Generally, people have difficulty remembering more than five key points. When preparing your session, write out the five most important things you want them to take away from the meeting. Create your presentation around these five items, ending with your most important one.

TIME

Keep a small clock where you can see it (but no one else). Try to eliminate your audience's (or client's) awareness of time during your presentation.

When moving to a break, give your participants an odd time to return to their seats. "Be back by 10:46 ½" is more memorable than "Be back at 10:45".

Post the time to return on your flip chart.

Deliver content in 45 - 60 minutes segments...then give a review or take a break.

PRESENTATION BASICS

WHAT vs. HOW

At the end of the presentation, ask yourself, "How do I know that learning has occurred?"

How much time are you spending on your subject - the WHAT, versus HOW you are presenting it? Try to spend 50% on each. You may be the top expert in your field but unless you can deliver your information skillfully and with an understanding of adult learning concepts, you won't be able to successfully transfer your information to your audience.

Are you "presenting to forget" or is your audience "learning to remember"? Make your material simple. Simple to understand, simple to remember and simple to use.

"If you continue to do more of what you have already been doing, then you will have more of what you already have."

USING JARGON

Know who is in your audience - are the words you are using familiar to everyone?

Every meeting or presentation has jargon (vocabulary specific to the industry). Be careful how you use jargon as it can be confusing if not everyone in the meeting is up-to-date with new terms. If they are not, stop and explain the jargon as you come across it.

If, despite your best efforts, a lot of jargon or other technical terms are being used, have a way of posting the words and their definitions in a visible place such as a storyboard or flip chart for those who may not be familiar with them.

PRESENTATION BASICS

128

ASK WHAT, NOT WHY

"What Questions" is a great technique that you can use whenever you need to collect objective data from a group (employees, customers, team members, etc.)

Step 1

On a 3x5 card or Post-it® note pad ask your participants to write down 3 answers to <u>general</u> questions beginning with the word "What" such as:

- ◆ "What are the 3 most important functions of my job?"
- ◆ "What are 3 of my greatest personal (or professional) assets?"
- ◆ "What are the 3 greatest challenges you have with _____?

  With customers, ask them:
  - ◆ "What are the 3 greatest assets of your current _____?"
  - ◆ "What are the 3 greatest concerns you have regarding _____?"

Step 2

Once they've written them down, ask them to prioritize their answers 1, 2, 3.

Step 3

Ask participants to discuss their first choices with each other. Have them choose a partner (dyad) or form small groups.

Step 4

Collect the cards or Post-it® notes - make it anonymous.

Step 5

Now that you have the process rolling, you can ask more specific questions based on your informational needs such as:

- "What 3 things could management/your supervisor do that would assist you with your job/project/training, etc.?

JUST THE FACTS...

Asking "why" often triggers an emotion-based, defensive response.

Asking "what" is a much more neutral question. It asks only for facts, not for reasons.

PRESENTATION BASICS

PRESENTATION BASICS

PERFECT QUESTION

- Ask your participants/customers:

  "What would make this a perfect _____?" (meeting, presentation, product, service, etc.) Have them write out their answers.

  OR

  "What part of our/your current _____ needs the most improvement?"

GETTING QUESTIONS FROM YOUR AUDIENCE

- Ask your participants to write their questions on 3x5 cards. Collect them before each break and review them after they return to their seats. For more on encouraging questions from your audience, see page 63.

USING FLIP CHARTS:

Rather than using 3x5 cards, you can ask questions, collect the responses on Post-it® notes and post them on a flip chart, white board or on the wall where they will be visible throughout the meeting. Ask your participants/customers for the reasons they are meeting with you, their goals, challenges, etc. Refer to them during the session and try to address the issues raised.

You can also use flip charts, whiteboards, etc. to post:
- learning agenda - morning and afternoon
- starting, ending and break times
- ground rules
- jargon or unfamiliar words

OR
- to create curiosity, ask a rhetorical question or make a visual impact

STORYBOARDING: As you progress through your presentation, tear off your flip chart pages and post them on the walls as a visual reminder.

PRESENTATION BASICS

PRESENTATION BASICS

MORE CREATIVE WAYS TO USE 3x5 CARDS

- Ask participants to write the one thing they valued or liked most from your presentation. Collect these cards and put them in a box. On days that you are feeling uninspired, pull them out and review them.

- Distribute red and green cards. Use them for voting. Yellow cards can be used for "I don't know".

- Have them write down their 3 best ideas from your meeting/presentation as a take away reminder.

- Preprint the key points from your presentation or meeting on 3x5 cards. Give them to participants on their way out the door. Color code cards based on different subject/topic areas.

"RESPONSIBLE PERSON" TECHNIQUE

At the beginning of a workshop, ask for a designated "responsible person" at each group table (to hand out materials, speak for the group, etc.). Change the responsible person throughout the session.

Make it fun! Small groups can choose their "responsible person" by shoe size, length of time with the company, longest hair, etc.

Have the current responsible person choose the next responsible person by tapping the shoulder of another person in their group.

PRESENTATION BASICS

WIIFM

No, it's not a new radio station. It stands for What's In It For Me? It is a reminder to you that your audience is mainly interested in things that concern them.

Why are they here? Are they here because they have to be? Are they motivated and glad to be attending? What do they want to get from the presentation/meeting or from you? What are THEIR objectives?

Adults like to see theory applied to practical problems that relate to them. Make sure they leave the room with something they believe is *valuable* for them to have learned.

WIIFM

Your audience (client, team members, sales force) wants to know how they can apply the new information in their personal and/or professional lives.

- Give them examples and scenarios in which they can apply the information
- Give them reasons why they need this information
- How can they benefit?
- How can they use it?
- How will this work for them?

Then, ask them to give you more reasons why they think this would make their lives, jobs, etc. better or more interesting.

PRESENTATION BASICS

DEALING WITH DIFFICULT PEOPLE

Occasionally, you will have an individual in your audience who presents a challenge to you as the speaker. He or she may be side-talking and laughing loudly, making contrary statements or, in general, just doesn't want to be there. Here are a few ways to diffuse the situation:

- Involve them. When they are involved with you, they will be less likely to act out on their own.

- Move them. Often the offending party is sitting near people he or she knows. Have your attendees "count off" and then, regroup! Move the group that now contains the offending party to the front of the room.

- Make them the leader of a small group interaction. Technique: "Okay, whoever has been with the company the longest, will be the small group leader at their table." Make sure the criteria you use will actually make them the leader of their group.

  - Stand near them to deliver the training - all eyes will be on them as well as on you.

CLOSING

When you close your presentation you can accomplish several things:

- Review your key points one more time (based on the 6 times rule...see the next chapter on reviews).
- Ask for final questions from your client/audience. Clear up any remaining concerns.
- Tie the learning/information to personal applications (affective memory) to help anchor it into long-term memory. Remember that the learning has taken place in the artificial world of the training/presentation room. Your audience/client needs to have real world applications if he or she is to use, apply and remember the information.

An effective closing makes your entire session memorable.

PRESENTATION BASICS

CLOSING TECHNIQUE - BRAIN DUMP

At the end of your presentation, ask for 2 volunteers to come to the front of the room. Using 2 flip charts (or extra sheets taped to the walls) ask the volunteers to write down the ideas that will be generated during the exercise.

Hand a small ball to someone in the audience. Ask them to call out an idea or concept from the presentation and then toss the ball to someone new. As the ball is passed around, each person holding the ball calls out another idea or concept. Participants can "pass" if they can't think of anything - you want to keep the pace brisk. The ball is tossed until everyone is finished calling out ideas. The idea is to have the audience "dump" all of the ideas/concepts/information from the session in a fast-paced, stream of thought process.

CLOSING TECHNIQUE - BRAIN DUMP cont.

When all of the ideas have been called out (and this exercise may generate as many as 150-200 ideas based on the length of your session), thank your volunteer scribes and your audience for participating.

After the Brain Dump is over, save the flip chart sheets to compile a written list of all of the ideas generated. Mail or e-mail the list to your participants 30 days later as a post-presentation review.

Congratulate and thank your participants for attending.

PRESENTATION BASICS

PRESENTATION BASICS

DO YOU KNOW?

- Our average thought speed is between 800-1,000 per minute. We can listen at 700 words per minute and speak at 200-250 words per minute.

- 33 million business presentations are made every day.

- Most managers have never received any presentation coaching.

- People will always have questions. It is up to you to find out what they are.

- The best way to break a habit is to drop it.

DO YOU KNOW?

- You can momentarily increase the intelligence of your audience by sending oxygen to their brain. Have them take a few deep breaths. Get them laughing or moving.

- Your participants are more tired at the end of the day because of the day-long underoxygenation of their brains and the strain of having to think!

- 70% of our weight is on our spine while we are sitting. Getting your audience OFF THEIR 70% (getting them to MOVE) helps oxygenate their brains, increasing attention.

- People will unconsciously stop breathing when they are under stress or experiencing high excitement. If your audience or client is not moving or laughing, make sure they are breathing....

PRESENTATION BASICS

PRESENTATION BASICS

DO YOU KNOW?

◆ People are more likely to participate if they are seated closer together. Get your audience to move together and remove any empty chairs before you start.

◆ Learning begins when you say, "I don't know". Getting your learners to say, "I don't know" opens their minds to all sorts of new possibilities.

◆ According to Network and MCI conferencing, 91% of meeting participants admit to day-dreaming during all or part of a meeting.

◆ People who voluntarily attend a training or presentation do so for only two reasons: They want to increase their knowledge or build their skill levels.

DO YOU KNOW?

- We send ourselves 40,000 - 60,000 messages each day with our internal self-talk (yes, this number is absolutely accurate). Of those statements, roughly 96% are negative. So lighten up and give yourself a break!

- Collaboration reduces stress and creates a positive learning environment. Studies have shown that groups create 80% more ideas than individuals working alone.

- Our minds tend to think in visuals - we see the object in our minds, rather than the words so paint pictures for your audience of your key points. Be descriptive.

There are two types of people - those who come into a room and say, "Well, here I am," and those who come in and say, "Ah, there you are."

- Frederick Collins

Chapter 8 - Reviews

WE LEARN BY DOING...

"I hear, I forget! I see, I remember! I do, I understand!" Confucius, 453 B.C.

Aristotle once said, "What we learn to do, we learn by doing". Learner/audience involvement increases retention - the more they do, the more they remember and the greater the impact on long-term memory.

Make your reviews (and all of the learning) FUN! If you can trick your brain into thinking it is having a good time rather than learning, it will do amazing things!

THE SIX TIMES RULE

MEMORY AND RECALL. According to studies completed at UCLA, your listener's long-term retention of the material can be increased to 90% by reviewing the information **6** times*.

Obviously, to repeat the same thing verbally six times would be terribly boring! So, to assist your audience (or client) in remembering the learning, use creative ways to review the information at least six times before, during and after your meeting or presentation.

Send an e-mail or fax ahead of time with your agenda and/or a brief outline of what you are going to cover.

> After your meeting or presentation, distribute job-aids to use, follow-up with a phone call, or send them a 30-day review fact sheet.

*Albert Mehrabian, Ph.D., Professor Emeritus, UCLA

REVIEW TECHNIQUES

During the meeting or presentation, making your review sessions interactive also keeps mental alertness, energy levels and attention high. Say it, show it and have them participate.

- PowerPoint/Overheads
- Handouts
- Storyboards
- Have them take notes
- Give it to them in a review or as a post test
- Let them teach each other what they just learned
- Give them take-away job aids, brochures, questionnaires or marketing material

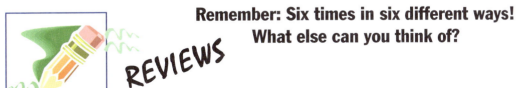

Remember: Six times in six different ways!
What else can you think of?

REVIEW TECHNIQUES

● Have a middle or end-of-meeting review. Be creative...use puzzles, games, question and answer sessions, etc. Have the participants tell you what they've learned so far.

● Dots, Post-it® flags and highlighters are visual attention-grabbers and curiosity stimulators. Use them in different colors and in a variety of ways when reviewing.

● Review the material using scenarios in which your learners can apply the information in their personal lives.

Ebbinghouse Forgetting Curve - We forget 50% of what we have just learned unless we use it right away.

REVIEW TECHNIQUES

- TEAM TEACHING EXERCISES
  At the end of your session, hold a teaching exercise in which participants teach others what they've just learned, particularly if they will need to explain it to others afterwards. You will know your audience "got it" if they can teach it!

- YESTERDAY / TODAY REVIEW
  If a training session continues for more than one day, have a quick review of the previous day's material at the beginning. Follow this with a quick pre-session preview of what is going to be covered in the current day's session.

- BRAIN DUMP
  At the end of the session, facilitate a "brain-dump" exercise (see page 138).

MORE REVIEW TECHNIQUES

- MIND MAPPING
  Create a mind map of your presentation and give to participants as a take-away. You can find more information on creating mind maps at www.mind-map.com.

- IDEA DRAW
  Or better yet, ask participants to draw their best ideas and/or what they have learned on a blank sheet of paper at the end of the seminar to create their own mind map. They don't have to be a Michelangelo - basic drawing skills are just fine. Using visuals, words, numbers, sequence and randomness combine to create a powerful review technique.

Mind maps double retention and help create a culture of creative learning!

MORE REVIEW TECHNIQUES

- ACTION PLANNING
  At the end of a presentation review on **paper** (visual stimulation) what the immediate next steps are going to be. Indicate what actions or recommendations can be deferred until a later time. Remember, "seeing is believing".

- 3X5 CARD BEST IDEA MAIL-BACK
  At the end of the presentation hand out 3x5 cards and a blank envelope which they self-address. On the card, have them write down their 3 best ideas from the presentation, place it in the envelope and seal it. Collect the envelopes. Mail them 30 days afterwards for a 30-day follow-up review.

REVIEWS

POST-PRESENTATION REMINDERS / JOB AIDS

● Industry specific jargon can be used as a post-presentation reminder. Create a jargon sheet with icons and definitions to send to the client as a follow-up to the meeting.

● Have key points preprinted on 3x5 index cards. Give them to clients or participants for quick reference. Color code the cards based on different subject areas.

● Make your handout memorable even after you have left the meeting by making it usable as a reference piece or job-aid.

● Create a take-away page containing the key points from your presentation or meeting. Make it colorful by using colored card stock and/or clip art. Laminate and distribute a copy to everyone who attends. (A double-sided, half-sized sheet will reduce lamination costs.)

Chapter 9
One-on-One (client interviews)

One-on-one situations can be more challenging than presenting to a large group. There is nowhere to hide and precious little you can do to cover your mistakes. You have to know your material inside and out - and know how to present it well.

Many of the same techniques for presenting to a larger group are also applicable with one-on-one sales or prospecting interviews. Adult learning issues such as safety and ownership, use of visuals, retention and attention techniques, accelerated learning theories, etc. are even more important when working one-on-one or in small groups.

The following techniques will give you methods to increase rapport and involvement with your client and create a buying environment.

ONE-ON-ONE client interviews

CHOOSING A LOCATION

Often, you have no choice in choosing a location for your meeting, particularly if it is an internal or small group meeting.

However, when meeting with outside clients or prospects one-on-one, try to arrange to meet them outside their office. This way you do not have to compete with the piles of work in their in-baskets, the telephone, secretary, e-mail, or other interruptions that can (and will) occur.

Another reason to avoid meeting in your client's office is that you will be on his home turf there - meaning you will be the outsider. By moving the location to a more neutral place, even if it is just down the hall in a conference room, the playing field will be a little more balanced.

Be aware of potential distractions in the room itself. Avoid rooms with windows or near busy hallways. Is it quiet? Will there be people moving in and out?

ROOM SETUP

SEATING. If you are in control of the room setup, and are meeting at your location, have a choice of seating arrangement, (both formal and informal) if possible. Your clients will feel more comfortable if they can choose where they sit. Avoid sitting at the head of the table or behind your desk, use a round table if one is available.

Is there space in the room to move the chairs around? Do the chairs have wheels? Your kinesthetic clients will be less restless if they can move around, even slightly.

A/V. If you have equipment to set up or materials to unpack, it may be easier to set up in a conference room down the hall in advance of inviting your audience/clients in for the start. This way you won't waste their time while you get ready and it creates a more dramatic first impression.

ONE-ON-ONE client interviews

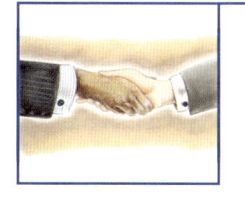

ONE-ON-ONE client interviews

156

BODY LANGUAGE

Body language and eye movement can be one of your best guides to determine if your presentation is going well.

If your clients look or act interested, confused, pleased, bored or restless they probably are. Based on their unconscious signals, change the focus/direction of your presentation, speed up the pace or slow it down, review key points or take a short brain break.

Someone who is interested, excited and engaged in your presentation will speak up during a pause - to ask questions, share ideas, etc. If your client is content to let you do all the talking, you should try another angle or move on to another topic that is more interesting to them.

Make eye contact with your clients. It sends the message that you are interested and focused on them.

BOUNDARIES - A QUICK REVIEW

Boundaries are extremely important in one-on-one interactions - so important that a quick review of the key points is in order:

- Watch for the body language cues of your client
- Be aware of your own body language
- Be a mirror:
    - Adopt your client's body language (if it's positive)
    - Adopt your client's tone of voice and enthusiasm (upbeat, excited, calm, etc.)
    - If their body language is negative, keep yours neutral
- Avoid the visual power position - get to equal eye level or lower

ONE-ON-ONE client interviews

ONE-ON-ONE client interviews

BEFORE THE APPOINTMENT

You can establish a buying psychology in your client before the meeting by mailing, e-mailing or faxing:

- A short questionnaire about his or her current conditions and goals

- The agenda - ask the client to add or remove items

- Send two 3x5 cards to your client and ask for the best/worst conditions of his or her current program/system/product. Ask them to bring the cards to the meeting. Start the meeting by discussing the cards

Also remember to send a **confirmation** with the date, time and location and a few bullet points as a reminder of what you want to accomplish.

BEFORE THE APPOINTMENT

- Send a "light" marketing brochure about you and your services - include references. It gives the client something to read and touch.

- Send a list of required documents, instruments, statements, information, etc. that you need to prepare for the meeting.

- When marketing yourself to new clients, send letters of reference from individuals who are in the same career and/or income bracket. Third-party references from happy customers are your best source of feedback to a potential customer.

- Send a 4x8 notepad and highlighter pen and ask the client to bring them to the meeting. The notepad and pen should always have your name and phone number imprinted on it.

ONE-ON-ONE client interviews

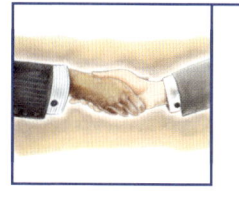

ONE-ON-ONE client interviews

"WHAT" QUESTIONS TECHNIQUE

The "What Questions" technique is an extremely valuable method that can also be used in one-on-one presentations. At the beginning of your meeting, ask your client to write 3 responses to questions such as:

- ◆ "What are 3 reasons you have purchased this product/service in the past?"
- ◆ "What are the 3 most important qualities in a vendor?"
- ◆ "What are the 3 biggest changes in your business since our last sales call?"

The answers will give you a foundation to start your meeting. And by having the client write, you get the client engaged in your presentation.

WHEN IN DOUBT - HAVE THEM WRITE IT OUT!

"WHAT" QUESTIONS TECHNIQUE

Remember to use the:

"Perfect" question -

"What information do you need to make this a perfect _____?

"Greatest Challenge" question -

"What is the greatest challenge that you have with _____?"

"Greatest Strengths" question -

"What are the three greatest strengths of your _____?"

ONE-ON-ONE client interviews

ONE-ON-ONE client interviews

At the:

BEGINNING of the meeting, ask your client, **"What would you like to learn today?"**

DURING your meeting have a visual chart that represents all of the written text of your recommendations. Ask your client to prioritize the importance level of each decision that was made during the meeting.

Make sure you give your client enough brain breaks - ideally, one every 8-12 minutes. Even a slight change in focus will stimulate attention and improve retention. Keep your client involved!

At the:

END of the meeting, review any remaining primary concerns.

DID YOU KNOW?

The average salesperson spends 10% of any day in front of potential clients and 57% of the day either eating or driving!

USING "DOTS" and POST-IT® FLAGS

Self-sticking "dots" are available at office supply stores in packages of assorted colors and sizes.

Ask your client to highlight certain areas of their handouts or other materials by placing a "dot" or Post-it® flag on the pages of their handout to mark:

- what they need to act on now
- what they want to act on later
- what needs a decision (and if not by them, by whom?)

ONE-ON-ONE client interviews

ONE-ON-ONE client interviews

USING "DOTS" and POST-IT® FLAGS

Ask your client or participants to highlight specific areas of their handout. Give them Post-it® flags or small, self-sticking dots to mark the pages with different colors...

- Red = "I don't understand this at all!"
- Yellow = "I'm a little confused."
- Green = "This is great!"

At the end of the presentation go back to the marked sections to review and answer questions. Ask them what makes certain sections so easy for them to understand and others more difficult.

CUSTOMER INVOLVEMENT - AFTER THE MEETING

You have an opportunity to create a higher level of customer involvement if you send a:

- "Next Steps" plan of action/responsibility page 15 days after your meeting
- Customer satisfaction questionnaire (keep it short - no more than 5 minutes in length) 30 days after your meeting
- Referral questionnaire based on the customer satisfaction response 45 days after your meeting
- "Next Steps" program outline 90 days after your meeting

ONE-ON-ONE client interviews

ONE-ON-ONE client interviews

MORE WAYS TO KEEP THE CONTACT ALIVE

◆ Send a letter immediately to the client you just left. Have the majority of the letter written ahead of time so that you can add the final touches and e-mail, fax or overnight it as soon as you get back to your office. This is a letter about them....make it relevant to their interests, not yours.

◆ Send a special marketing gift, based on the degree of the customer's action/commitment, 60 - 90 days after the sale.

◆ Send birthday, anniversary and children's birthday congratulations. Do you know the name(s) of your customer's spouse and/or children?

   ◆ ALWAYS send a thank you note to the individual who referred you.

Chapter 10
Lifelong Learning Principles

These 7 Lifelong Learning Principles can motivate, change perceptions, increase results and change lives as well as improve your performance as a presenter and the performance of your audience members. Each one could fill a book chapter, but since that is not the intent here, a very brief introduction to each is included. How you use them is entirely up to you.

**Have banners made proclaiming all 7 principles.
Hang them in your presentation room for added emphasis.**

LIFELONG LEARNING PRINCIPLES

UP TO NOW

Use these words when someone in your audience, (or employee, child, spouse) says they have a challenge or a problem. It shifts them to a "solution mode" and away from staying in the problem. Explain that everything in their life can be an "Up to Now" moment if they choose.

An employee may say, "I don't understand what my supervisor wants." You can add, "Up to now." This is not meant to be a flip answer, but a psychological reframe designed to change that person's perception of the problem. It is an opportunity for opening the door to the possibility of a different outcome and an extremely powerful, motivating statement that will initiate the change process.

WHAT IS

The current health (individual and organizational), wealth, state of relationships and education level are examples of your participants' personal "What Is" factors. The important thing to understand is that it is the reaction to the circumstance or event that affects an individual's overall success, failure, happiness or dissatisfaction. The same applies on an organizational level.

A presenter should ground his or her presentation in reality, addressing the "What Is" issues of the organization. Acknowledge legitimate concerns, business conditions and make the session relevant for your audience.

LIFELONG LEARNING PRINCIPLES

LIFELONG LEARNING PRINCIPLES

BE HERE NOW

In other words, be present. Are you present in your mind and body? Is your mind somewhere else in thought? Where are your participants? Are they in an aware, learning frame of mind and body?

There are 4 stages of Being Present:

- ◆ Physical
- ◆ Mental
- ◆ Emotional
- ◆ Self-esteem

BE HERE NOW - PHYSICAL PRESENCE
STAGE ONE

Sometimes just getting yourself and your audience physically present is a challenge. Often there are physical issues that prevent individuals from focusing on the task or discussion at hand. Acknowledging these issues and generally providing an environment that promotes physical well-being will eliminate physical distractions.

You can help your participants remain physically present in your session by giving them adequate time to check and return phone and e-mail messages, take a necessities break, eat lunch, etc. Make sure the room set-up, temperature and seating are comfortable.

LIFELONG LEARNING PRINCIPLES

LIFELONG LEARNING PRINCIPLES

BE HERE NOW - MENTAL PRESENCE
STAGE TWO

Being mentally present means getting into the right frame of mind, being alert and participating in what is happening right now. When your audience members are not mentally present, learning cannot occur. If you are distracted, it affects your presentation.

A simple method of bringing your audience (or yourself) back to mental awareness is to do something physical. Being physically and mentally present are tied closely together, so get your participants to move (even slightly) to get their blood flowing, get them to laugh or give them something different to look at.

BE HERE NOW - EMOTIONAL PRESENCE
STAGE THREE

If a participant is under emotional stress (external or internal), he or she will "check out" of the present and "check in" to sadness, anger or depression. Instantly, their reality becomes a negative emotional state. While in this state, the brain signals the body to release chemicals that are dispersed to numb the individual's mind and body. High levels of efficiency and learning are difficult.

As a presenter you can not know or predict who in your audience is in a negative emotional state and you certainly cannot be expected to solve their problems. But, getting your audience emotionally involved during your presentation will help them be here now.

Remember, the more emotionally attached your listeners are to your material, the more they will remember it.

LIFELONG LEARNING PRINCIPLES

LIFELONG LEARNING PRINCIPLES

BE HERE NOW - SELF-ESTEEM PRESENCE
STAGE FOUR

The highest level of being present, or being here now, is the level of self-esteem. If self-esteem is high and the participants are generally happy with their lives, they will have a tendency to be more present and in the moment.

The concept of self-esteem can be expanded from the individual to include an entire organization. What is the current workplace environment like? Are spirits high? Are people functioning at a positive and effective level? As a presenter, make your session a contributing factor in raising the self-esteem levels of participants. Acknowledge the accomplishments and successes of team members, individuals and the entire organization.

I AM ENOUGH

Now comes the principle of "I am enough". It is being comfortable with who you are and not seeking external approval for your beliefs, actions or self-worth.

As a presenter, when you believe that you are enough you can focus on your audience, what they want/need to learn and on delivering the learning without being concerned with whether they will like you or agree with what you have to say.

Take feedback from your participants as an opportunity to improve your skills - being aware that your participants will focus on the one or two things they did not like about your presentation (and most will be eager to tell you about them) rather than on what they did like.

LIFELONG LEARNING PRINCIPLES

LIFELONG LEARNING PRINCIPLES

I DON'T KNOW

Have you spent any time today in a state of "I don't know"? It really is where learning occurs! When we say, "I know", we close ourselves off from new ideas and solutions or possibilities to our challenges. When you catch yourself saying "I know", refocus yourself into the mindset of an "I don't know" learner. You will open your mind up to a host of new possibilities!

Likewise, the best place for your audience to be is in a state of "I don't know" where solutions can be discovered, old paradigms discarded and new points of view developed.

> **Learning does not occur when you say, "I know", learning only occurs when you say, "I don't know."**

I, YOU, WE, ALL

This concept is the least tangible of all 7 principles. It is an examination of 4 levels of awareness, both individually and organizationally. On an individual level, it is a reflection of how your participants interact, participate and learn by themselves and as a group. Being aware of an organization's level can give you some valuable insights into potential areas of growth and change, directing you to where the most work may be needed.

The 4 levels are:
1. I - focused inwardly on own needs
2. You - focused on creating relationships, gaining acceptance
3. We - focused on larger community impact
4. All - focused on global issues, contribution to society

LIFELONG LEARNING PRINCIPLES

LIFELONG LEARNING PRINCIPLES

I

It may sound unusual to say that an organization has an "I" personality. But an "I" organization is one which may be newly established, looking for a niche in the industry or a way to define their uniqueness. They are focused inwardly, developing their internal structures and establishing their place in the industry.

When focused so intently on their own goals, an "I" organization may seem to be insensitive to the needs of its employees or the community at large. The greatest asset of an "I" organization is its capacity for creating new and innovative ideas and products. They are often the bright new stars on the business horizon.

They are perfect candidates for marketing, product branding or technical and product development training programs.

YOU

With a "You" focus, an organization is beginning to build its customer relationships and create a solid internal work environment. In a professional context, it makes good sense to nurture and develop employees at this time, providing them with adequate training in both hard and soft skills. The motivation behind a "You" organization is creating a solid business foundation to support the creative ideas and products that have been launched. It is a time of internal and external relationship building - serving the needs of both customers and employees.

A "You" organization is a good candidate for customer service training programs, as well as sales, interpersonal and communication skills seminars.

LIFELONG LEARNING PRINCIPLES

LIFELONG LEARNING PRINCIPLES

WE

For most organizations, long-term success comes as they evolve towards a "We" philosophy. Moving beyond "I" and "You", an organization will begin to focus on workplace and leadership issues and their profile in their own community.

Internal "We" relationships include those between employees and management, various departments, and team members.

At this stage, team-building, leadership development, delegation, time management, supervisory skills, communication and interpersonal skills are often what is needed to promote continued organizational strength and growth.

ALL

"All" is a consciousness that extends beyond the organization and into a more global awareness. Organizations may be rethinking their core mission, vision and values, and working on balancing the needs of employees, the company, their community and the environment.

Training programs should be designed to incorporate the application of hard and soft skills in both the employees' work and home environments. Training departments can become learning centers and a resource for the betterment of the community. Organizations may sponsor community service programs and encourage employees to participate.

Lifelong learning is part of the corporate culture. Leadership skills are of key concern as well as developing interactive exercises and tools designed to promote objective feedback and future planning.

LIFELONG LEARNING PRINCIPLES

LIFELONG LEARNING PRINCIPLES

FROM NOW ON

Once your audience has grasped "Up to Now", and you've had the "Up to Now" banner hanging in the room during the first phase of your session, take it down and replace it with one that says, "From Now On".

"From Now On" is the point of change - the moment moving forward in which the decision and commitment is made to change the "Up to Now" results. "From Now On" is where action plans are made, and frankly, it is where the rubber hits the road. If "Up to Now" is the recognition of unlimited possibility and new outcomes, then "From Now On" is the real work of creating results. Take your audience into an interactive experience of what they can accomplish "From Now On" and give them the tools they need to achieve their goals. Presentation follow-up, mentoring programs, job-aids, etc. can create successful "From Now On" results.

Additional Resources - print

Armstrong, T., **7 Kinds of Smart: Identifying and Developing Your Many Intelligences**, New York: Penguin Books, 1993.

Brood, Mary & Newstrom, John, **Transfer of Training**, Addison-Wesley, 1992.

Buzan, E.P., **Use Both Sides of Your Brain,** E.P. Dutton, Inc., 3rd Edition 1991.

DeBono, **Lateral Thinking: Creativity Step by Step**, Harper & Row, 1990.

De Porter, Bobbi, **Quantum Learning**, Dell Publishing, 1992.

Dellinger, Susan, **Communicating Beyond Our Differences. Introducing the Psycho-Geometrics System™**, Jade Ink, 1996.

Gardner, Howard, **Frames of Mind, the Theory of Multiple Intelligences**, Basic Books, 1983.

Hoff, Ron, **I Can See You Naked,** New, Revised Edition, Andrews and McMeel, 1992. (training techniques)

Hoffman, Edward, **Psychological Testing at Work, How to Use, Interpret, and Get the Most out of the Newest Tests in Personality, Learning Style, Aptitude, Interests and More!**, McGraw Hill Professional, 2001.

Jensen, Eric, **Brain-Based Learning**, The Brain Store, Revised Edition 2000.

Knowles, Malcom, **The Adult Learner**, Gulf Professional Publishing, 5th Edition 1998.

Meier, Dave, **The Accelerated Learning Handbook**, McGraw-Hill, 2000.

Russell, Peter, **The Brain Book**, Penguin Books, 1979.

Scannel, Edward & Newstrom, John, **More Games Trainers Play**, McGraw-Hill, 1983.

Additional Resources - websites

Conferences and Other Learning Resources:

Center for Accelerated Learning	www.alcenter.com
Creative Education Foundation	www.cef-cpsi.org
International Alliance for Learning	www.ialearn.org
International Alliance of Facilitators	www.iaf-world.org
American Society of Training and Development	www.astd.org
The Ned Herrmann Group	www.hbdi.com
Buzan Centres	www.mind-map.com
Lifelong Learning Partners	www.jackwolflearning.com

Other Sites:

Training Magazine	www.trainingmag.com
Trainer's Warehouse	www.trainerswarehouse.com

BE HERE NOW - EMOTIONAL PRESENCE
STAGE THREE

If a participant is under emotional stress (external or internal), he or she will "check out" of the present and "check in" to sadness, anger or depression. Instantly, their reality becomes a negative emotional state. While in this state, the brain signals the body to release chemicals that are dispersed to numb the individual's mind and body. High levels of efficiency and learning are difficult.

As a presenter you can not know or predict who in your audience is in a negative emotional state and you certainly cannot be expected to solve their problems. But, getting your audience emotionally involved during your presentation will help them be here now.

Remember, the more emotionally attached your listeners are to your material, the more they will remember it.

LIFELONG LEARNING PRINCIPLES

LIFELONG LEARNING PRINCIPLES

BE HERE NOW - SELF-ESTEEM PRESENCE
STAGE FOUR

The highest level of being present, or being here now, is the level of self-esteem. If self-esteem is high and the participants are generally happy with their lives, they will have a tendency to be more present and in the moment.

The concept of self-esteem can be expanded from the individual to include an entire organization. What is the current workplace environment like? Are spirits high? Are people functioning at a positive and effective level? As a presenter, make your session a contributing factor in raising the self-esteem levels of participants. Acknowledge the accomplishments and successes of team members, individuals and the entire organization.

I AM ENOUGH

Now comes the principle of "I am enough". It is being comfortable with who you are and not seeking external approval for your beliefs, actions or self-worth.

As a presenter, when you believe that you are enough you can focus on your audience, what they want/need to learn and on delivering the learning without being concerned with whether they will like you or agree with what you have to say.

Take feedback from your participants as an opportunity to improve your skills - being aware that your participants will focus on the one or two things they did not like about your presentation (and most will be eager to tell you about them) rather than on what they did like.

LIFELONG LEARNING PRINCIPLES

LIFELONG LEARNING PRINCIPLES

I DON'T KNOW

Have you spent any time today in a state of "I don't know"? It really is where learning occurs! When we say, "I know", we close ourselves off from new ideas and solutions or possibilities to our challenges. When you catch yourself saying "I know", refocus yourself into the mindset of an "I don't know" learner. You will open your mind up to a host of new possibilities!

Likewise, the best place for your audience to be is in a state of "I don't know" where solutions can be discovered, old paradigms discarded and new points of view developed.

> **Learning does not occur when you say, "I know", learning only occurs when you say, "I don't know."**

I, YOU, WE, ALL

This concept is the least tangible of all 7 principles. It is an examination of 4 levels of awareness, both individually and organizationally. On an individual level, it is a reflection of how your participants interact, participate and learn by themselves and as a group. Being aware of an organization's level can give you some valuable insights into potential areas of growth and change, directing you to where the most work may be needed.

The 4 levels are:
1. I - focused inwardly on own needs
2. You - focused on creating relationships, gaining acceptance
3. We - focused on larger community impact
4. All - focused on global issues, contribution to society

LIFELONG LEARNING PRINCIPLES

LIFELONG LEARNING PRINCIPLES

I

It may sound unusual to say that an organization has an "I" personality. But an "I" organization is one which may be newly established, looking for a niche in the industry or a way to define their uniqueness. They are focused inwardly, developing their internal structures and establishing their place in the industry.

When focused so intently on their own goals, an "I" organization may seem to be insensitive to the needs of its employees or the community at large. The greatest asset of an "I" organization is its capacity for creating new and innovative ideas and products. They are often the bright new stars on the business horizon.

They are perfect candidates for marketing, product branding or technical and product development training programs.

YOU

With a "You" focus, an organization is beginning to build its customer relationships and create a solid internal work environment. In a professional context, it makes good sense to nurture and develop employees at this time, providing them with adequate training in both hard and soft skills. The motivation behind a "You" organization is creating a solid business foundation to support the creative ideas and products that have been launched. It is a time of internal and external relationship building - serving the needs of both customers and employees.

A "You" organization is a good candidate for customer service training programs, as well as sales, interpersonal and communication skills seminars.

LIFELONG LEARNING PRINCIPLES

LIFELONG LEARNING PRINCIPLES

WE

For most organizations, long-term success comes as they evolve towards a "We" philosophy. Moving beyond "I" and "You", an organization will begin to focus on workplace and leadership issues and their profile in their own community.

Internal "We" relationships include those between employees and management, various departments, and team members.

At this stage, team-building, leadership development, delegation, time management, supervisory skills, communication and interpersonal skills are often what is needed to promote continued organizational strength and growth.

ALL

"All" is a consciousness that extends beyond the organization and into a more global awareness. Organizations may be rethinking their core mission, vision and values, and working on balancing the needs of employees, the company, their community and the environment.

Training programs should be designed to incorporate the application of hard and soft skills in both the employees' work and home environments. Training departments can become learning centers and a resource for the betterment of the community. Organizations may sponsor community service programs and encourage employees to participate.

Lifelong learning is part of the corporate culture. Leadership skills are of key concern as well as developing interactive exercises and tools designed to promote objective feedback and future planning.

LIFELONG LEARNING PRINCIPLES

LIFELONG LEARNING PRINCIPLES

FROM NOW ON

Once your audience has grasped "Up to Now", and you've had the "Up to Now" banner hanging in the room during the first phase of your session, take it down and replace it with one that says, "From Now On".

"From Now On" is the point of change - the moment moving forward in which the decision and commitment is made to change the "Up to Now" results. "From Now On" is where action plans are made, and frankly, it is where the rubber hits the road. If "Up to Now" is the recognition of unlimited possibility and new outcomes, then "From Now On" is the real work of creating results. Take your audience into an interactive experience of what they can accomplish "From Now On" and give them the tools they need to achieve their goals. Presentation follow-up, mentoring programs, job-aids, etc. can create successful "From Now On" results.

Additional Resources - print

Armstrong, T., *7 Kinds of Smart: Identifying and Developing Your Many Intelligences*, New York: Penguin Books, 1993.

Brood, Mary & Newstrom, John, *Transfer of Training*, Addison-Wesley, 1992.

Buzan, E.P., *Use Both Sides of Your Brain,* E.P. Dutton, Inc., 3rd Edition 1991.

DeBono, *Lateral Thinking: Creativity Step by Step*, Harper & Row, 1990.

De Porter, Bobbi, *Quantum Learning*, Dell Publishing, 1992.

Dellinger, Susan, *Communicating Beyond Our Differences. Introducing the Psycho-Geometrics System™*, Jade Ink, 1996.

Gardner, Howard, *Frames of Mind, the Theory of Multiple Intelligences*, Basic Books, 1983.

Hoff, Ron, *I Can See You Naked,* New, Revised Edition, Andrews and McMeel, 1992. (training techniques)

Hoffman, Edward, *Psychological Testing at Work, How to Use, Interpret, and Get the Most out of the Newest Tests in Personality, Learning Style, Aptitude, Interests and More!*, McGraw Hill Professional, 2001.

Jensen, Eric, *Brain-Based Learning*, The Brain Store, Revised Edition 2000.

Knowles, Malcom, *The Adult Learner*, Gulf Professional Publishing, 5th Edition 1998.

Meier, Dave, *The Accelerated Learning Handbook*, McGraw-Hill, 2000.

Russell, Peter, *The Brain Book*, Penguin Books, 1979.

Scannel, Edward & Newstrom, John, *More Games Trainers Play*, McGraw-Hill, 1983.

Additional Resources - websites

Conferences and Other Learning Resources:

Center for Accelerated Learning	www.alcenter.com
Creative Education Foundation	www.cef-cpsi.org
International Alliance for Learning	www.ialearn.org
International Alliance of Facilitators	www.iaf-world.org
American Society of Training and Development	www.astd.org
The Ned Herrmann Group	www.hbdi.com
Buzan Centres	www.mind-map.com
Lifelong Learning Partners	www.jackwolflearning.com

Other Sites:

Training Magazine	www.trainingmag.com
Trainer's Warehouse	www.trainerswarehouse.com

About the author . . .

A dynamic and highly respected speaker, trainer and consultant, Jack Wolf has specialized in the delivery of programs designed to provide performance solutions to clients since 1976. He has designed and presented programs on workforce learning, sales, creativity and performance improvement and has been a featured speaker at numerous conferences around the globe.

His techniques have been used with great success by many clients and course participants. Jack is a member of the International Alliance for Learning, Creative Education Foundation, Society of Insurance Trainers and Educators, Professional Speakers Guild and American Society for Training and Development.

Jack's articles have appeared in such publications as Training & Development, Successful Meetings, National Underwriter and Financial Planning News.